Let's explore together the pieces of the puzzle of the "All Knowing"

By rushordertees.com/blog/August 3, 2016 stock photo

"ALL KNOWING"
(The Omniscient God)

by

KEVIN FRANCIS O'CONNOR

EQUIP PRESS
Colorado Springs, Colorado

ALL KNOWING
(The Omniscient God)

First Edition: Year 2018
All Knowing: The Omniscient God / Kevin Francis O'Connor
Paperback ISBN: 978-1-946453-23-5
eBook ISBN: 978-1-946453-24-2

ABSTRACT

How does an all-knowing God reveal himself to a humanity that doesn't believe any longer in a Supreme Being? He left us communication through the ages using a medium called Prophecy. As the accuracy of these divine messages are being proven, a new level of intimacy with God is the result.

kmoconnor910@gmail.com

Dedicated to my wife Mindy and the ARK Church prayer partners.

The power of our team doing life together, whether in marriage or church, makes it a sweet journey.

Contents

Foreword   11

1. You Know My Inmost Being   15

2. Following Biblical Pieces   25

3. Jesus the Prophet?   47

4. Guardrails for Prophetic Scripture   63

5. Mysteries within the Jewish Feasts/Festivals   77

6. Healing a Broken Culture   95

7. The Bible within the Bible   107

8. A Prophetic Word   119

9. Keys to the Final Puzzle (Revelation)   133

10. The Christmas Prophet   153

11. Sleeping Beauty (The Church)   163

12. Beyond Literature   175

FOREWORD

Knowing

K *nowing* is a 2009 science fiction movie featuring Nicolas Cage, who plays John as an astrophysics teacher. His wife died in a tragic accident, and it has left him as an unbeliever. The story starts in 1959, with a student, Lucinda Embry, hearing whispers while staring at the Sun. When her idea to make a time-capsule is chosen by the school, each child draws what they believe it will be like in the future. Lucinda writes a page of seemingly random numbers for the time capsule, which is to be opened in fifty years. Lucinda's teacher calls for the pupils to finish, but Lucinda continues until her teacher takes the page off her desk.[1]

Fifty years in the future, Caleb, who is John's son gets Lucinda's letter when the time container is opened. His assignment is to write an essay about what they found in the capsule. His dad, John, is a professor at MIT. He notices that his son's letter from the capsule contains numbers in a set of sequences. The digits refer to the dates and death tolls of disasters over the last fifty years, including 911012996, representing the

---

[1] *Knowing,* (2009, Columbia Pictures), Knowing Fan Site.

date and death toll for the 9/11/2001 attack, where 2996 people died. The final three sets of digits on the page are dates in the immediate future. Warning, major spoiler alert! The last group of numbers deals with the ending of the world through a solar flare, which destroys all life. In the last scene, John goes to his father's house, who is a Christian and a pastor. They reconcile after all the years of disagreeing about God and his knowledge and how life plays out. They embrace as the solar flare hits, and the world ends in one big explosion.

We relate to the character Nicolas Cage plays, who wants real answers. The letter he received contained certainty about the future; everything came to pass with total accuracy. Are the letters we have from God as reliable and precise? Yes, because he knows the end from the beginning (Isaiah 46:10). Consideration of this truth is the first step to strengthening your faith in the truth of the Scriptures.

Let those who have an ear hear. Those words are spoken six times in the Gospels and eight times in Revelation. Mark Batterson preached a message on his latest book, *Whisper,* saying he believes there is a Catholic ear, a Baptist ear, a Pentecostal ear, a liberal ear, a conservative ear, a male ear, and a female ear. We all hear through different filters. [2]

Mark Batterson is right when he says there is also a theological ear. It will filter your view of God and his omniscience! God knows how to speak in every language and to every tribe. He talks to me through two different filters more than any other— my holy ear and my prophetic ear. I've learned there isn't much

---

[2] Mark Batterson, "Whisper," (sermon, Oct. 29, 2017).

to say to people if they don't sense the spirit of God when I am speaking. To communicate this way, I must first learn to hear his holy voice. In the same manner, to speak with a prophetic voice, I must have a prophetic ear. I have no problem hearing other authors, teachers, and preachers or sharing their view. But when I speak something God put into my heart, there is a whole new level of intimacy and power. The primary way to hear from God is through his Word.

His Holy Word has filters—cultural filters, reasoning filters, and tradition filters. Scripture itself is the primary filter of Scripture, while all the other helps make sure we are listening correctly. Scripture expounding on itself gives us the truth meter and insight, keeping us from faulty interpretation. The Holy Spirit is an excellent author, and his presence within the Word of God makes it timeless. Using other tools without Scripture as a means of interpretation makes the Scripture static. Locking Scripture in the ancient culture or tradition is theologically wrong. Even our reasoning can confine Scripture to our knowledge, which is limited. We must keep Scripture from being viewed as dead. Yes, within the Bible, there is culture. We do apply our reasoning skills and church tradition as tools. But what sets this book apart from all other books is the author. He is the all-knowing God who reveals his power that is living and active and sharper than any two-edged sword.[3] The Bible presents the author when it says all Scripture is God-breathed.

Did you notice how the character John in our movie uses his skills in astrophysics to solve the puzzles in Lucinda's fifty-year-

---

[3] Hebrews 4:12 NIV

old letter? In real life, the Holy Spirit led Isaiah to write a letter to a world leader, King Cyrus, 150 years before he was born. This letter also guided the prophet Daniel to give it to King Cyrus. In the scroll of Isaiah 45, he reads about his role to the nation of Israel and the temple. Cyrus amazingly trusted Isaiah's writings and helped the temple to be rebuilt. This and many more stories like them prove our God is all-knowing. Let's go on a journey together and discover the Word of God through the eyes of the omniscient one.

CHAPTER 1

You Know My Inmost Being

Psalm 139:13
For you created my inmost being;
you knit me together in my mother's womb (NIV)

Fathoming a Creator who knows everything is very difficult. He's asking the finite mind to do more than embrace the infinite but to trust it at the same time. There is nothing that takes God by surprise. God not only knows you, he sees and understands things about you that you might not figure out for years. His knowledge about you goes beyond the number of hairs on your head; he understands your hopes and desires. His all-knowing ability cannot be fully grasped. But, as we learn what the scriptures say about the omniscient God of the Bible, our faith will be anchored in that knowledge.

Weaving

Weaving is an art, and it has been around since the beginning of recorded history. We see evidence of it scripturally in Genesis. I love the story of Joseph's coat of many colors as an example of a woven garment. With skilled hands, our eternal ingredients are intertwined inside each child developing in the womb according to Psalm 139. David's DNA had a helping hand in life, and the source of that advantage was God. It seems like such an audacious statement, but can its validity be applied to every human being? The more I researched, the more the answer became clearer; yes, God is tucking unique potential inside every child while in their mother's womb.

Ethel Waters is a gospel singer, Academy Award-winning actress, and author of "His Eye Is on the Sparrow." In her autobiography, she describes how she came into this world because of a rape. Jesse Jackson, Presidential candidate, speaker, activist, and pastor—along with James Robinson, television evangelist, and Rebecca Kiessling— felt their lives were tainted as they were all conceived through the act of rape. Rebecca was terrified she would inherit her father's evil streak. The fear of having children, especially boys who could grow up with her father's genes, scared her. Today, she has a website about the many men and women who have and are changing our world. The common thread is they are here because of rape.[1] God, in his all-knowing ability, works his will and plan even when we face life's darkest situations. Everything in life cannot be classified as good, but when given over to an all-knowing God, he can work it for good.

David became the man he was because God put those ingredients inside of him. God knew he could slay giants; it was in his genes. He was born with the strength to kill a lion with his bare hands because he was a protector of the sheep. Everything

---

[1] http://www.rebeccakiessling.com/other-conceived-in-rape-stories/ famous-people-who-were-conceived-in-rape/

we learned about this shepherd boy, who rises to royalty, originated with the mixing of his father's seed and his mother's egg. King David was knitted together by God and nourished for nine months in his mother's womb.

All-Inclusive God

You, too, were knitted in your mother's womb. The kind of person you become involves more than your life's circumstances. David wasn't the family's recognizable choice for King. His brothers were experienced soldiers who were more prominent, more mature. But God told Samuel the prophet to anoint David. He was not a candidate for royalty from a human perspective. God was working in David's life before he took his first breath. How did the prophet know David was the right choice? The prophet Amos provides the answer. "For the Lord GOD does nothing without revealing his secret to his servants the prophets.[2]

Knitted into Samuel's inmost being was the ability to receive the secrets of God and obediently carry them out as the prophet of God. I am confident God is still weaving ingredients into children while in their mother's womb.

Notice God does the same for the prophet Jeremiah as he did for King David in Psalm 139 (NIV). "The word of the LORD came to me, saying, 'Before I formed you in the womb I knew you before you were born I set you apart; I appointed you as a prophet to the nations.' 'Alas, Sovereign LORD,' I said, 'I do not know how to speak; I am too young.' But the LORD said to me, 'Do not say, "I am too young." You must go to

---

[2] Amos 3:7 NIV

everyone I send you to and say whatever I command you. Do not be afraid of them, for I am with you and will rescue you,' declares the LORD. Then the LORD reached out his hand and touched my mouth and said to me, 'I have put my words in your mouth." Jeremiah 1:4-8 (NIV)

Some may view what's happening in the womb as unusual. What God is doing is an all-inclusive act, even though you might not be called to be a King like David or a prophet like Jeremiah. God did something for you as well. The Creator knitted eternity inside of you by giving you a soul. He placed his stamp or image inside of you while you were in your mother's womb. Your inmost being is your soul; it either responds to God or rejects him. There is a paradox in the concept of being created in God's image. We are born separated from God because of inbred sin. The inbred sin is activated from birth; while the image of God remains dormant until salvation. All the potential is there but cannot be activated until the activator Jesus Christ comes into our heart and throws the switch. We are then born again.

Activation Mode

In the Old Testament, the Holy Spirit activated the person's soul from outside the body. Today, it is an inside job. Parents, your role is more significant than donating your DNA to your children. Taking time to have devotionals, prayer, and God moments with them awakens their inmost being. Raising them in church creates yet another environment for them to experience the presence of God. But don't miss the role God is playing in this whole process. The following Scriptures give us his active role.

1. **Psalm 139:13** God is creating and knitting.

2. **Amos 3:7** God is revealing secrets to his servants.

3. **Jeremiah 1:4-9** God is forming you, God is setting you apart, God is putting his words in your mouth.

God is doing the work. As Christians, we play a role in the lives of others. But each person is ultimately responsible for the image they live up to. The good news of the gospel was accomplished for you before you were aware of it, and the power to achieve is given by the Spirit.

Christians, when they invite Jesus into their hearts, are allowing the knitting process to continue. Now the inside job occurs while you're learning how to walk, talk, and live a kingdom life. I am still learning how to incorporate God's kingdom into my life. But just like babies need to be fed and have their diapers changed, so do young Christians. They are not perfect. When Christians are adults physically and a baby spiritually, and they mess up, don't shame them. Just help them clean up. A spiritual newborn does not look much different than a non-Christian. But the knitting process has begun. Being born again will affect your mind, heart, and your strength for God. It also introduces you to where his kingdom resides. Neither shall they say, 'Lo, it is here!' or 'Lo, it is there!' For behold, the kingdom of God is within you."[3]

Being created in God's image has a community element—you are born into a family called the church. Individuals like David, Amos, and Jeremiah make up the body of Christ. We also

---

[3] Luke 17:21 KJV

call it the family of God. We are children of the King. We are co-heirs with Christ in this mighty kingdom. God is revealing his secrets to the church. God is forming his church, setting us apart, and giving us his words. He is making a bride for his son without spot or wrinkle. Celebrating what God is creating in our inmost being is the beginning of worship. Sin creates a significant distortion in our ability to spiritually discern. Jesus established the church to protect us from sin, falsehoods—a community who helps each other with the gift of holiness. Christian can be an example of God's Holiness.

The Helpers

My role is two-part—pastor/prophet within God's kingdom. There is still a little fear and trembling to say God called me to be a prophet also. Most Americans don't understand the office of a prophet and often relate the word prophet to a cult—showing a lack of knowledge about the five-fold ministry. Paul's epistle taught us about church leadership. "So Christ himself gave the apostles, the prophets, the evangelists, the pastors, and teachers, to equip his people for works of service, so that the body of Christ may be built up."[4] Jesus, like God the Father, is the Creator. We call Jesus's creation the church. He created within the church helpers or servants that would prepare followers for service. No human being or organization started the church. He's been knitting it together from the first century. Apostles are people sent out; we call them missionaries in most church circles. Surprisingly, second on the list are the prophets and

---

[4] Ephesians 4:11-12 NIV

prophetesses in their roles of watchers. Evangelists are those who proclaim the gospel. Pastors are the leaders of the community in daily life. Teachers are the educators; all five positions have a role in the educational process. The goal stated in Ephesians is to build up the body of believers in the knowledge of God's kingdom. We don't often hear about where or how a person receives a call to be a prophet. Here's how it transpired in my life.

A Prophet Is Knitted

My story was woven together in a township outside of Philadelphia called Collingdale. My home was an old twin home built in 1910. The house was the only one we called home. But Mom would say, "Oh, if these walls could talk." One evening, during college break, Mom said, "I have a word to share with you." Something was different in her tone of voice. She said, "There's something I've needed to talk to you about. Since the day I heard about God talking to you and a Scripture in Jeremiah, well, frankly, as your mother, I've been conflicted. But I didn't want you to know what I had done." She continued, "There's an Irish tradition in our family you need to know. The first male child born would be named after their grandfather." The second male child born is named after the father.

She confessed, "I didn't care for your grandfather and swore I would never name any of my children after Charlie." She went on, "If I hadn't rebelled against the family tradition, your brother Jeremiah O'Connor Jr. would be Charles O'Connor and you being the second child would have the legal name, Jeremiah, after your dad."

Being called by God was not by chance. It wasn't an accident I found that Scripture. It was God's ordained circumstances. Since learning of my spiritual identity, mom's words have been a source of strength and comfort in my journey. A quantum leap in confidence was the result. Venturing into my newfound identity, I read everything I could on the prophets.

God has a way of knitting life together. Interweaving an Irish Catholic with a call to follow Jesus in a Nazarene church has its unique moments. It is all part of shaping this pastor/prophet's holy life. Through the years I've been asked whether there is a significant difference between Catholics and Protestants. Wanting to answer positively, I state how they are alike. But some friends are persistent, so I redirect their focus with the following question: Do you know the difference between Catholic holy water and Protestant holy water? The reply was always an inquisitive, "no." I would then explain how Catholics make their holy water by blessing it. The Protestants take a much holier approach. They boil the hell out of it. (That joke was shared with me by a dear friend and partner in ministry who is now in heaven. Thank you, Pastor Eugene Breinig.)

My journey became a passionate, in-depth, ongoing learning experience about this all-knowing God. My Catholic upbringing planted the clear picture of a God who is everywhere, knows everything, and can do anything. Combining it with the experience of a Holy God, I can say I am experiencing new levels of a holy life in acknowledging God's role in my inmost being.

Writing has become a new part of this adventure. Friends asked me to write about the interpretation of prophetic Scriptures from a Wesleyan perspective—to share how prophetic Scripture constitutes a significant part of the scriptural picture, to arm them with clues they aren't finding in our ministerial circles. They are asking the hard questions: Is the Bible God's message system? If so, is there a "Morse Code" for the Scriptures? Are there still prophetic Scriptures to be answered?

Chuck Missler, author, and Bible teacher says, "The Bible is an integrated message system."[5]

My secret of retaining great truths and letting them get into my soul is to add a twist to the original, creating a new unique statement. **"The Bible is a** divine **integrated message system."** Forty authors wrote the Bible over fifteen hundred years. But as Chuck will tell you, one author is behind it all, The Holy Spirit. A God-centered life leads to a holy life in him. Only wanting to give him a small or remote part of your life will make you a religious person. My journey is not a religious one; it is wholly relational.

One role of the prophet is to be a watchman or watchwoman—crying out a warning about perceived dangers in our world. General Booth of the Salvation Army did this very thing over a hundred years ago.

---

5   Chuck Missler, "A Message from Outside of Time," (2013).

> "The chief danger that confronts the coming century will be religion without the Holy Ghost, Christianity without Christ, forgiveness without repentance, salvation without regeneration, politics without God, heaven without hell."
>
> ~William Booth[6]

I will add to William Booth's concerns about a worldview whose designer is not God. A biblical worldview is the key to the Christian movement and the Holiness movement. How many decisions are you making based on your biblical worldview? If you cannot name any choices you've made in the last year based on a biblical worldview, then you don't have a biblical worldview. You only have a biblical opinion. Opinions never change people. The Bible does and has changed millions and will continue to do so.

---

6   General William Booth, Sermon Quotes, Salvation Army.

CHAPTER 2

Following Biblical Pieces

Psalm 33:4 (NIV)

For the word of the Lord is right and true; he is faithful in all he does.

God is faithful; this premise is about his exactness. Therefore, it cannot be he's mostly right or most of the time true. With God, 100 percent right and true is a non-negotiable in his essence. God desires for us to know him, so he gave us revelation knowledge about him tucked away within the Scriptures.

If you love God, you must embrace the vastness of his character and how he manifests it to humanity. We cannot pick or choose which parts of God we will accept and which we will reject. The Holy Spirit reveals the attributes of God. Here is a non-exhaustive, alphabetized list:

The spirit of gentleness
The spirit of holiness
The spirit of joy
The spirit of love

The spirit of justice
The spirit of kindness
The spirit of mercy
The spirit of peace
The spirit of power
The spirit of prophecy
The spirit of wisdom
The spirit of wrath

God loves puzzles

Think of the Bible as a six-thousand-piece puzzle. Each piece holds information, history, culture, experiences, wisdom, and timeless wonder. They connect to the other parts, forming a clear picture of the kingdom of God. Have you ever taken the time to do a puzzle? If so, did you ever get near the end and discover pieces are missing? My wife's mom, Vivian, loves puzzles. At her house, you can see her table set up in the corner of the living room with her latest project. She once said she never buys a puzzle at a garage sale because of a chance a piece is missing. In the same way, imagine God putting thousands of years into his Word and then not have the parts match, connect, or the meaning clear. A warning to not mess with his puzzle comes in the book of Revelation. Society is guilty of adding to his picture of the marriage puzzle. In doing so, it has distorted its view. Genesis puzzle pieces give civilization a clear picture, by connecting the image of a holy and all-knowing God to the world.

Genesis to Revelation is a narrative about God. It is also about civilization's journey from creation in Genesis to the re-creation of the heavens and earth in Revelation. Before God creates, we see a piece of his all-knowing nature in his love and plan called grace. Before the foundation of the world, the Lamb of God was slain.[1] Before the groundwork was laid, before Adam and Eve sinned, Jesus was the answer. Call it prevenient grace. The gift of grace is a window into God's will and an ultimate gift for all humanity.

> **Prevenient grace** *is a Christian theological concept rooted in Arminian theology, though it appeared earlier in Catholic theology. It is divine* **grace** *that precedes human decision.*[2]

Prevenient grace is God's love for us before we knew him. The doctrine of prevenient Grace is a fundamental ingredient when it comes to salvation. Without grace, we cannot be saved. If salvation is attached to anything other than the unmerited favor (grace) of God, we could boast about it. We cannot be good enough, kind enough, or faithful enough to earn our way into grace. The border pieces of a puzzle command everything else to be inside of them. Prevenient grace works as the border of salvation. All provision for a Christian life comes after grace. My professors taught us to see prevenient grace in every chapter of Genesis and how it connects to the big picture of grace. "For it is by grace you have been saved, through faith— and this is not from yourselves, it is the gift of God."[3]

> It is divine grace that precedes human decision.

---

[1]   Revelation 13:8 NIV

[2]   https://en.wikipedia.org/wiki/Prevenient_grace

[3]   Ephesians 2:8 NIV

Sequential thinking is paramount when it comes to grace as God's provision. Faith is appropriating the endowment grace has bought. Faith is the mechanism by which I receive the endowment. My belief doesn't move God to do something on my behalf. It only activates what's been done. My grant remains in the heavenly university until I apply for it through faith. It can go unused. Jesus is the one who set up this trust fund for humanity. Before you were born, the prearrangement for your needs were made. The gospel is the good news about a gift. It's waiting for you to accept it.

The Picture on the Box

Good puzzle people look at the shapes of the pieces. They notice the uniqueness of a curve or an edge of the piece. The average puzzle person studies the picture on the puzzle box and separates the pieces by the colors seen in the picture. Great puzzle people, like Vivian, use all these techniques. Her secret is to have good lighting when putting it all together. The Bible is **the light** for our path.[4]

In the same way, prophecy, creation, and the book of Genesis are essential for lighting the full picture of salvation. Each piece is connecting a part of the image. The creation story lights up the background of sin—answering the questions what is it and where did it originate?

As a Christian nation, we understood this light, and it was common knowledge for a long time. The average person on the streets knew about the Ten Commandments. We grew up

---

4   Psalm 119:105 NIV

knowing we needed Jesus for salvation. Adam and Eve's fall didn't have to be explained. Most understood sin as a concept. Maybe not its origin, but they knew enough to steer clear of anything we called sin. In school, if we talked about God, they recognized him as the Creator.

Many Christians are not aware of these biblical pieces today. The essentials of the faith aren't critical pieces any longer to this generation of believers, nor to this present culture. A different picture of life has become their narrative. Biblical illiteracy is growing among Christians because of false doctrine. The latest poll among evangelicals tells us 60% of Christians believe everyone makes it to heaven.[5] This is a direct result of clergy not being a guardian of the truth. We don't want to attack each other, so we look the other way and we are suffering because of it. Most students today couldn't solve the simple puzzle chart in the diagram below, so I've supplied the answers on the next page.

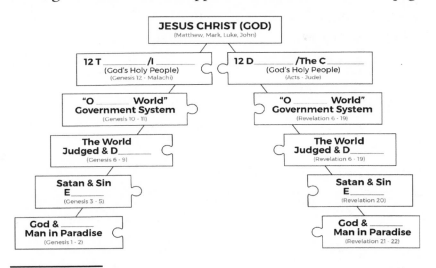

---

[5] G Shane Morris, "Survey of Christians," (Oct. 10, 2016).

This chart came from 12 Stone Church, and it is a great tool to show the pieces of the Bible do fit together. **Answers:** Righteous, enters, destroyed, one, tribes/Israel, disciples/Church, one, destroyed, exits, redeemed [6]

The Bible fits the beginning pieces to the end of the story flawlessly. God's overall plan for humanity fits together in a way that no one should miss the connections. Psalm 18:30 — "As for God, his way is perfect: The LORD's word is flawless; he shields all who take refuge in him."

> **Proverbs 30:5** – *"Every word of God is flawless; he is a shield to those who take refuge in him.*

The essentials of the first eleven chapters of Genesis connect with the last chapters of Revelation. It is only possible because the authentic author of the Bible is the Holy Spirit. If you don't accept the importance of the beginning of the book, you won't ever figure out the end. Our charted diagram pieces connect the Bible in its entirety. Could a random event have done this? God orchestrated the details. Biblical specifics give astounding demarcation to our developing sketch. Wow, what a picture it is going to be.

The Creative Puzzle

The first inventions and their inventors are found in Genesis before the flood. Shared wisdom and creativity over

---

[6] Pastor Kevin Myers, "The Bible," (sermon, 12 Stone Wesleyan Church, 2011).

a more prolonged lifespan had some real advantages. Fathers are passing on valuable insight to their sons. The genealogy of Genesis has always fascinated me. It's more than just a list of Hebrew names. Living alongside each other for more than 500 years brought a richness of shared experiences and insights. Only the Bible gives us that kind of history. We get glimpses of what it was like leading up to the flood—their names and how they connected with the Creator. Their contribution gives us a "cool peek" at the biblical puzzle. Genesis 4:19-22 – "Jabal was the father of those who live in tents and raise livestock. His brother Jubal was the father of all who play the harp and the flute. Tubal-Cain, who forged all kinds of tools out of bronze and iron."

Theologians and scientists tend to dupe us into thinking the old world was filled with dumb, ignorant humans living in caves. But the Scriptures reveal responsible ranchers, tool makers, and even inventors of musical tradition. These were all passed down before Noah's flood. Music is not my forte, but praise team personnel over the years have taught me a lot. My attention is drawn to Jubal—the father of all who play the harp. Now, how curious do you have to be to invent a harp? Where did he find the pieces to put together this instrument in the period before Noah's flood?

*Strings for harps are usually made of either **nylon**, gut (or **synthetic** gut), wire, or a combination thereof. Celtic (folk, lever) harps are most often strung with **nylon** or wire; classical (pedal) harps are usually a combination* *of* **nylon** *(high end), gut or* **synthetic** *gut (mid-range), and wire-wound (bass).*[7]

Two weeks ago, I heard Erwin McManus speak on this section of Genesis. I laughed at his message title because of the timing in my writings. "God shares his creative powers with us."[8] I am building on Erwin's truth—we are co-creators with God. Following his reasoning about inventors in 3983 B.C., here are some conclusions. There was no nylon or synthetic wire in existence. Jubal found catgut! I imagine, like most boys, he likely encountered a cat whose misfortune was being a partial dinner for another animal. Imagine him looking inside the feline abdomen and dissecting the cat's gut; that's what boys do. In pulling on it, yep, the harp was the next puzzle piece in place. Like Hansel and Gretel, our God is leaving us clues. Each logical step guides us to his eternal plan.

It All Starts with Genesis

Genesis is called the book of beginnings. Foundational truth is at its very core. These fundamental truths go beyond sin, man's fall, and God's grace. There's marriage, the devil, deception, and the birth of Israel. But let's stick to the pieces we already know for a little longer. When Paul was preaching to the Jews, they didn't need foundational teaching. They grew up understanding the law and the consequences of sin and the price of sin. So, when sharing the gospel, he could cut to the chase and point

---

[7] https://en.wikipedia.org/wiki/Catgut

[8] Erwin McManus, (sermon, February 15, 2016).

them directly to Jesus the Christ—the missing piece of their lives and the Messiah of the world. 1 Corinthians 1: 23-24 – "But we preach Christ crucified: a stumbling block to Jews and foolishness to Gentiles, but to those whom God has called, both Jews and Greeks, Christ the power of God and the wisdom of God."

He didn't fulfill their desire to overthrow the Roman Empire. Jesus is foolishness to the Gentiles and the Greeks because they haven't discovered any foundational truth. They need the doctrines of Genesis. The gospel sounds foolish if you don't know about sin. Gentiles and Greeks are lost on the simplicity of the New Testament gospel. Ask what God they are referencing, and you will get different answers. To the Muslim; God is Allah; to the Buddhist, God is Buddha; and the Hindu has so many gods we couldn't name them all. We must take Paul's approach, laying down a foundation as he did for the Greeks at Mars Hill. Acts 17:23 – "For as I walked around and looked carefully at your objects of worship, I even found an altar with this inscription: TO AN UNKNOWN GOD. So, you are ignorant of the very thing you worship—and this is what I am going to proclaim to you." The God who made the world and everything in it is the Lord of heaven and earth. He does not live in temples built by human hands. The God of the Bible has become the unknown God of our society. A generation that has little truth, or worse, a view of a tainted Bible. The believers who trust in the Bible to direct their worldview is shrinking at alarming rates. The Bible's purpose is to set the worldview. Sadly, some use Scriptures to support a distorted view. The Bible rarely shows up on their radar as the trendsetter.

Ken Ham said: *"We need to turn our culture from a Greek cultural world back to a Jewish world.*[9]

Society is a Greek cultural system with many gods. The system made its way into the church, and its pluralistic worldview; everyone does what is right in their own eyes. It affects the way people look at the Bible. If their worldview is to thrive, they must attack the foundations of Genesis. New believers need encouragement about the validation of Genesis. If given all the tools to make a proper decision, can Christians maintain a biblical worldview? Clarity about sin must be based on God's Word. The absolutes about sin are eroding, but its consequences are growing. Living together, homosexuality, and multiple sexual partners is the norm. Emphasis on psychology, biology, and social norms override biblical knowledge. The erosion of morals is escalating so fast people learn about each other's bodies intimately before they know the person's last name. What was once a no-brainer, a natural snap together pieces of the moral puzzle for one generation is lost in another age while the crowds shout for more liberties. Total freedom is another word for anarchy.

The building blocks of the first eleven chapters of Genesis is vital in bringing people to Jesus. The Creation story has become a significant resource for understanding a scriptural belief system. At this juncture of history, the Bible could have made its way to China. Rediscovering Genesis may reach millions or billions of people. It could be the missing link to a whole people group who don't know the gospel.

---

[9]   Ken Ham, "Acts 17, Evangelism" Answers in Genesis, June 12, 2004.

The China Connection

I love the pieces of a puzzle with a solid color. When they are blue, we look to see if they fit in the sky. Green for grass, dark blue for water, white for clouds, and yellow is often for the sun. In our world puzzle, two-color pieces could represent over a billion people. Welcome to the yellow and red parts of our picture.

The color **yellow** is a symbol of earth. This color, is very important in Chinese symbolism, representing glory, wisdom, harmony, happiness, and culture. **Yellow** is reserved for the Emperor. A **red** envelope is a symbol of prosperity. **Red** is also the color of **Chinese** weddings, representing good luck, joy, and happiness. Thus, **red** should not be worn to funerals. Yellow/gold is considered the most beautiful color.[10]

Mindy and I became empty nesters for about three days. Our daughter Hannah left for Point Loma Nazarene University, and then the phone rang. There was an emergency at our Christian School concerning two international students arriving in three days without any host parents. The question? Were we willing to take two girls—a 9th-grade student and a 10th grader into our home and life? It would be a commitment for the next ten months! Their English was limited, but they could understand more than they could speak. A long-term adventure was birthed. We reached a new culture like missionaries while living right in our home. Genesis became the key to us introducing them to Jesus.

My son Shawn; his wife Haley; and our grandchildren Ethan and Micah were living in China, teaching English as a

---

[10] George Allen, "Color in: What do they mean?" (January 17, 2011).

second language in Beijing. Shawn sent us a YouTube video (https://www.youtube.com/watch?v=DA-AkJzpKmg)[11] on the Historical language of the Chinese. The Pastor gives a detailed explanation of their written ancient dialect. It was so beautiful, with all kinds of symbols and characters taken from Genesis! 2,500 years before Buddhism, Confucianism, and Daoism, the Chinese worshipped a singular god. His name was Shangdi, and it means *the Most-High God*. Within their symbols and their language, was an undeniable connection with the concept of the Most-High God. Their historical symbols include a garden experience identical to Genesis. They have a story of deception about two trees through a false revelation from a serpent, and sin entered their world. The two trees are the tree of life and the tree of knowledge. Their symbols are also telling the story of a famous flood and Noah's Ark. Grade school children learn to draw the symbols for a large boat. It is a drawing of a boat, plus the symbol for the number eight. Why? In Genesis, the large boat had Noah, his wife, their three sons and their wives—the eight survivors of a world flood. These truths enable us to see how important the creation story is to the most massive people group on the planet, the Chinese. We now show the video each year to our Chinese guests; it's sending them home with God's foreknowledge and love. Christian schools in the inland-Empire have agreed to use this video. The international and American students in Bible classes are learning the foundational truth of the Genesis account.

Historians believe Noah's son Shem went east after the flood. Shem's creative way of reaching the Chinese people with their

---

[11] https://www.youtube.com/watch?v=DA-AkJzpKmg

historic language may be the best puzzle piece for these people. Until this knowledge reaches them, they will believe the Bible is a western religion. After seeing the video, they accept the Bible as their heritage.

SHEM, while it is Noah son's name, also means something personally to Mindy and me. Shawn, Haley, Ethan, and Micah were serving God in China. They are the source for this story and our learning about the video on the origin of the Chinese language. It was God's way of driving home His point.

Generational Pieces

For the next step, God's puzzle comes from a man named Abram. His name means exalted father. It took God two thousand years from the fall of Adam to select Abram. He will be the subject of a personal prophecy from God—a promise to change the world through him. God said, "You will be the father of multitudes." That translates into the name Abraham. Prophecy often has bugs to work out pointing to God's omnipotence. It was taking a long time for Abraham to have a single heir. God specifically said Sarah would be with child. She laughed over that because of her age. Abraham and Sarah decided to interpret the prophecy themselves. The custom of the day was that if your wife was barren, you would use a maidservant. Hagar became part of the equation. When we try to force God or a prophecy into our timetable or our understanding of it, we lose. Long-term ramifications can be the result. Abraham's decisions are felt today around the world. The descendants of Ishmael, is part of a conflict that has lasted now four thousand years in the Middle East.

God's omnipotent nature comes to the rescue. Sarah was barren, and Abraham was as good as dead.[12] They became parents to a boy they would name Isaac, which means laughter.

Isaac would be the grandfather of the twelve tribes of Israel. Understanding these twelve tribes is the core of the rest of the Old Testament. Abraham and Sarah took most of a lifetime to achieve God's will, but it was worth it because of the faith lesson learned. Future generations will point to this miracle and promises of God, and to Abraham as the focal point of the faith. Our lives also are meant to be a fulfillment of God's dreams. There is hope for us. Sometimes the vision takes a detour as we see in the twelve sons of Jacob.

A Difficult Puzzle

Jewish genealogy has been compared to learning to read a Hebrew phone directory. Difficult tasks will follow in assembling the pieces needed to birth the nation called Israel. Difficult does not mean impossible. It's often mind-boggling. Here's why some breakthroughs are so hard. People are a part of the equation making every outcome unique. We avoid hard things at all cost. We like stories that have easy narratives. Sub-plots in a story or movie will get lower ratings if they are hard to follow; we love simplicity. Well, not all people balk at complexity. Some enjoy a challenge, following the clues, connecting the dots. A faithful believer will eventually dig until they find the answers. Some answers may take a lifetime. The twelve sons of Jacob are more than a handful, but they are also an impressive group of men.

---

[12] Hebrews 11:11-12 NIV

Notable puzzle solvers are in it for the long haul. People who learn from the all-knowing God develop fortitude. Reinforcing God's truth becomes a way of life. The Jewish heritage puzzle is a piece of cake compared to what students did in Vietnam to get into the Guinness World Record. The jigsaw puzzle with the most pieces consisted of 551,232 pieces and was completed with an overall measurement of 48 ft. 8.64 in. x 76 ft. 1.38 in. by 1,600 students of the University of Economics of Ho Chi Minh City (Vietnam), at the Phu Tho Stadium in Ho Chi Minh City, Vietnam, on 24 September 2011. The jigsaw puzzle depicted a lotus flower with six petals in symbolic representation of the six areas of knowledge envisaged by the Mindmap study method. It took the students 17 hours to first break up the 3,132 sections, each containing 176 pieces, into which the jigsaw puzzle had been divided, and then reassemble them to create the puzzle.[13]

Wouldn't it be amazing if the Christian community could come together like these students? Each had to respect the other student's portion of the puzzle. They couldn't say to others, "We don't believe in your part of the picture. To complete more than a half a million-piece puzzle, someone had to know that it all would fit together. God knows how the Bible puzzle pieces fit; you could never imagine God starting a task and coming up a few pieces short.

The Family Puzzle

We now meet the twelve puzzle pieces that will make up the nation of Israel and the Jewish people. Think of them as the large

---

[13] Guinness World Record Book, (Sept. 24, 2011).

blended family that they represent. The order of their births is as follows: Reuben, Simeon, Levi, Judah, Issachar, Zebulun, Dan, Naphtali, Gad, Asher, Joseph, and Benjamin. These are the sons of Jacob the twelve tribes of Israel. The order of the sons' births increases the level of difficulty about the prophecy of the coming Messiah. He would be the son of David and from the tribe of Judah. Hebrew tradition states the birthright goes to the first born male of the family. Circumstances must change to allow Judah, the fourth born to receive that right. A story within a story unfolds, revealing God's acceptance of all people.

The first three sons, Reuben, Simeon, and Levi, all disqualify themselves. Judah is now positioned to receive the birth blessing. The genealogy stories in the New Testament reflect the many changes about to take place. Most people don't read that portion of the Bible, thinking it is boring. Each name tells a story. Each name is a piece of Israel's puzzle. Family skeletons are also hidden within those names. Judah's choices disclose how life's biggest mistakes can be used for God's glory. Yes, you can still be used by God, even after a huge mess up.

Jesus is called "the lion of Judah." Some puzzle pieces arrive at their spot only after much twisting, twirling, and turning. Once the birthright was secure, Judah would suffer along with the rest of us in a very personal sin. Romans 3:23 – "For all have sinned and fallen short of the glory of God."

Sordid Details

Aren't you glad your sins, mistakes, and failures aren't recorded in the Bible? The knowledge that every generation will read your shameful details shouldn't be a punishment.

The Christmas of 1975 was marked by my grandfather dying of cancer. He couldn't say no to alcohol during his lifetime. I arrived at the hospital to see Grandpa with so many questions on my mind. Would this be my first death experience within our family that I would remember? All families have stories they don't want aired in public. I had heard of deathbed confessions, and I was about to experience one firsthand. Grandpa told me of a young man in seminary in Pittsburgh, PA. He was studying to become a Pastor when he met my grandma Pearl. They fell in love, but she was only fifteen years old. Later, when my family learned of the news that a baby was on its way, they were devastated. Some sins are more than families can handle, especially when society is conservative. The shame of a teenage pregnancy out of wedlock by a seminary student was a real scandal in the 1930s. Well, that's how my mom came into this world. Add a three-hundred mile move to Philadelphia, a quick marriage, and a lost calling, and the weight of the world was now on a man facing death. Never having the opportunity to right that one wrong, he was sure hell was heating up for his arrival. Years of guilt told him what he deserved. When life is marred, can the pieces ever make sense? The world is hoping it can, for it needs a redeeming story it can trust.

Judah lost a son named Er because he was wicked. Scripture says God put him to death. Judah's second son was given to his daughter-in-law Tamar, because of Hebrew custom. Onan would, by proxy, help Er's name live on, fulfilling the law. He would accomplish this by giving his sister-in-law a child. If a son was conceived, Er's name and lineage would continue. Life would go on through his brother's seed. But Onan spilled his seed on the ground, preventing Tamar from conceiving. God saw what Onan did as wicked and put him to death.[14]

Now Judah was afraid to give another son to Tamar since he had lost two sons already. He denied his sons' wickedness and blamed Tamar for his loss. In Genesis 38, this story goes from bad to worse. Tamar disguises herself as a prostitute while Judah is in town. Judah sleeps with her, and she gets pregnant, with twins! When he hears his daughter-in-law is pregnant, he is irate and summons her to bring her to justice. She shows Judah the staff and the ring of the person who is the father of her children, and Judah realizes it is him.

The Forgiveness Piece

Judah, like my grandfather, didn't know what to do with his sin. I am here writing today because my grandmother and grandfather chose life for my mom. They could have swept her breath away with abortion.

Judah recognized his sins, not having enough faith to give his third son to Tamar. He acknowledged he was the father of her twin boys—Perez and Zerah. God poured out the power of his grace and forgiveness to Judah and Tamar. New Testament genealogy places this puzzle piece in a prominent place. Tamar remains single. Judah provides for her children financially. Her son Perez's bloodline becomes the bloodline of the Savior. So, when we say Jesus is from the tribe of Judah, it's packed with

---

[14] Genesis 38:9 NIV

sordid details and forgiveness wrapped together. Every generation needs this truth in Genesis. The more entrenched your sin goes, no matter how long you've stayed in your mess, the blood of Jesus goes deeper and further than the sin. His sacrifice on the cross paid the price for our sins in full, including the tip of future grace. The blood of Jesus is provision for all the past, present, and future sordid deeds.

Grandpa on his deathbed cried, repented, and accepted the good news that no stain goes deeper than the blood of Jesus. Isaiah was right when he prophesied, "Though your sins are like scarlet they shall be as white as snow." William Yuhas, the seminary student drop-out, is in heaven today as a testimony of grace. Judah's piece of the puzzle links us to Perez, his son through Tamar, and his future descendants will reveal another mystery.

The Missing Piece

What makes the Marvel comics so popular? Marvel's stories are filled with heroes, and young boys are naturally drawn to people with special powers. The attraction goes beyond their powers; it's the ability to protect the world from all kinds of evils. It's a winning formula for a hit movie. The Bible gives us real-life heroes who do save the day.

The Hebrew culture called them kinsman-redeemers. The tradition is a safeguard against tragedy. The nearest male blood relative is the Kinsman. Several essential obligations were transferred to the next of kin when death or other problems occurred. If poverty made them unable to redeem their land, it was the kinsman's duty to redeem it. He was also required to redeem his relative from slavery.

The book of Ruth is a connecting piece to our Genesis story, a traditional reading at harvest time during the Feast of Weeks, also known as Pentecost. It's a classic love story, and it's essential to the relative's puzzle piece. Interestingly, it will also link to Jesus.

Ruth's story is about the need of a kinsman, as we all do. Revelation chapter 5 reveals Jesus as the ultimate kinsman to the world. Why is John the apostle weeping in the story? Because there was no one worthy, no kinsman to open the scroll. The scroll represents the deed to the earth, lost when our first family sinned. Only a sinless Kinsman Redeemer can open the scroll/deed. Jesus had to become flesh to take up the role of the Kinsman. He is called the last Adam, the hope of humanity. Revelation 5:5 – "Then one of the elders said to me, 'Do not weep! See, the Lion of the tribe of Judah, the Root of David, has triumphed. He is the only one able to open the scroll and its seven seals.' In saying this, the angel points to the true Kinsman, who has just made all the pieces fit so we could see the association. Jesus purchased the deed to the earth with his blood.

Forming a Mosaic Puzzle

In the event of a husband's death, the family can continue to live without fear for their future because of the kinsman principle. It's the reality Naomi depends on for her tomorrow. Her opportunity comes in Ruth 3. She knows how this puzzle works. When her son died and left her with a daughter-in-law name Ruth, she knew what to do. Going home for Naomi was the only chance of finding a kinsman for Ruth. Boaz is the kinsman she finds. Her opportunity to regain the family properties is at hand. Ruth and Boaz fall in love with each other. Naomi instructs Ruth on how to proceed. The problem comes when Boaz informs them another kinsman is a closer relative than him, meaning Boaz would have to step aside. But if that family member was unable to fulfill his duty, either financially or relationally, then the role would be cleared for the next of kin. Boaz gets the news; the way is clear for him. He will be the one to redeem Ruth and marry her and take Ruth's mother-in-law Naomi into their extended family. Ruth 4: 11-12 – "Then the elders and all the people at the gate said, 'We are witnesses. May the LORD make the woman who is coming into your home like Rachel and Leah, who together built up the family of Israel. May you have standing in Ephrathah and be famous in *Bethlehem*. Through the offspring the LORD gives you by this young woman, may your family be like that of Perez, whom Tamar bore to Judah.' The blessing they received at their wedding was, **"May your family be like Perez, whom Tamar bore to Judah."** The Elders extend a blessing on them that would be famous in Bethlehem. Well, this perfect little romance has several critical redeeming facts. It connects the dots for us. It also gives us the insight into other biblical puzzle pieces. Once in obscurity but now completing a royal destiny. When one piece comes together, suddenly, many other pieces seem to fit, and this is what happens in our Old Testament story.

God's mosaic is gathering the pieces of broken lives.

Boaz's the Kinsman; his mother was a famous prostitute named Rahab.

Rahab, rescued for protecting the two spies, Joshua sent to Jericho.

Salmon, one of the two spies, marries Rahab.

Ruth, a Moabite. Her family tree includes (Genesis) Perez, his mother Tamar, his father, Judah.

Boaz and Ruth's first child is Obed. He will become the father of Jesse.

Jesse becomes the father of David the King.

Jesus Christ is born, son of David, and of the tribe of Judah.

A mosaic is broken pieces coming together to make a masterpiece. Also, this is how an all-knowing God creates his masterpieces, through broken lives that yield to his purpose. Jesus selected men like tax collectors, fishermen, and women that no one else would choose to weave a team of disciples together that changed the world.

CHAPTER 3

Jesus the Prophet?

Psalm 138:2
*"For you have exalted your Word
above all your name" (KJV).*

Jesus is called the carpenter, Rabbi, and Son of David, to name a few. He refers to himself as the bread of life and living water. God commanded us to honor his name. The Psalmist is telling us, that above his name is his Word. In the Old Testament, your name was only as good as your word. Let me introduce you to the Living Word, Jesus the Prophet. It frustrated me when other religions would refer to Jesus as a prophet, teacher, or a Rabbi, which is a teacher in the Jewish community. Was this a put down to the Son of God?

Out my childhood bedroom window, I could see across the street to the church of the Nazarene–their beautiful stained-glass picture of a life-sized Jesus. He's standing at the door and knocking.[1] When you open the door of your heart to Jesus the Savior, you also invited in the prophet, the teacher, and Lord

---

[1]   Revelation 3:20 NIV

47

into your heart. All of Jesus came into our hearts. I just couldn't comprehend what it really meant, but I was going to find out.

The Jews would not recognize Jesus as a suffering servant or as the Messiah. Israel only saw Jesus as a teacher/prophet. Their hope in a Messiah was one who would set them free from the Roman Empire. I dismissed Jesus's prophetic nature for a long time until he said unless I have all of him in my life, he's not Lord of it. This fact opened my mind to a new level of prophetic truth from the all-knowing God. Reading the words of Jesus after this acknowledgment changed what I saw and understood. It was as if I walked into certain passages for the very first time. Could there be a veil over Christians' eyes who don't see Jesus's prophetic nature? I only know that I felt like a veil had been lifted for me. Teaching these next several points is very challenging. If you only see surface views of what the Scriptures are saying, this may be very frustrating to follow. If you can grasp the following truths, you've gone to another level in the living and active Word of God.

Prophecy & Punctuation

Matthew 5:18 – For truly, I say to you, until heaven and earth pass away, not an iota, not a dot, will pass from the Law until all is accomplished (ESV). (This becomes a little like following the bouncing ball.)

1. Jesus assertion, about the punctuation in Scripture, is designed to give us a puzzle piece. This announcement is the clue concerning his first and second coming.

2. It's Jesus himself who changes the punctuation! You must first understand that while Jesus was reading the scroll of Isaiah out loud in the temple, he altered the reading.

3. He places a period in Luke 4:19 where there is a comma in the original passage in Isaiah 61:2.

4. This action becomes the fulfillment of his prophecy in Matthew 5:18 about the punctuation. Jesus is separating his first coming and what he would fulfill and his second coming by leaving out the phrase "the day of vengeance" through the punctuation.

Luke 4:18–19 *"The Spirit of the Lord is on me, because he has anointed me to proclaim good news to the poor. He has sent me to proclaim freedom for the prisoners and recovery of sight for the blind, to set the oppressed free, to proclaim the year of the Lord's favor."* **(Notice a period***)*

Isaiah 61:1–2 *The Spirit of the Sovereign LORD is on me, because the LORD has anointed me to proclaim good news to the poor. He has sent me to bind up the brokenhearted, to proclaim freedom for the captives and release from darkness for the prisoners* **(Notice a comma where Jesus put a period in Luke 4:19)** *2 to proclaim the year of the* **LORD's favor,** *and the day of vengeance of our God, to comfort all who mourn,*

After quoting Isaiah 61, Jesus declares it is fulfilled on that day. He did not cite all of Isaiah 61:1-2, leaving out the phrase "the day of vengeance," knowing it would not be activated until his second coming. The punctuation left the event in the future. The use of a period lets us see two ages being expressed. Commas are used as a pause in time. Jesus confirms his position as the God of the Bible. He fulfilled setting the captive free (the first advent); his punctuation change gives prophetic insight about the day of vengeance (the second advent season). Jesus created a ruckus with the announcement that he had fulfilled the Scripture. Prophets were known for producing commotions. But it had nothing do with his changing the scriptural text punctuation. He stirs up his hometown of Nazareth with truths from the Old Testament.

> Jesus is separating his first and second coming, with punctuation.

The incident in Luke 4 almost cost him his life, but not for the things mentioned. Jesus's teaching addresses Israel's false concept of God's love. Israel taught their children to rejoice over the death of a pagan because God was rejoicing. This perception of God is deep-rooted in lies from the devil. This false concept has crept into many world religions.

When Truth Gets You in Trouble

Luke 4:24-27 – "Truly I tell you," he continued, "no prophet is accepted in his hometown. I assure you that there were many widows in Israel in Elijah's time, when the sky was shut for three and a half years, and there was a severe famine throughout the land. Yet Elijah was not sent to any of them, but to a widow in Zarephath in the region of **Sidon.** And there were many in Israel with leprosy in the time of Elisha the prophet, yet not one of them was cleansed—only Naaman the **Syrian."**

Jesus, acting in a prophetic role, brought high levels of distress to his hometown. Acceptance was not Jesus's goal; he was there to serve his Father. Obedience is God's bottom line for every servant. The two short stories of Elijah and Elisha aren't popular Jewish narratives because of their endings. The Jewish leaders consider their history a source of pride bringing validation to them as special to God in their own eyes. The first story is about Elijah being sent by God during a great famine in all the land, including Israel; this isn't a pleasant reminder. Pointing out Elijah was sent only to a Gentile widow in Zarephath in the region of Sidon is rubbing salt in their wound.

The second story is about Elisha's power. Leprosy was a significant problem in Israel, destroying many families. But Elisha only cleansed one person of the disease, a man named Naaman the Syrian. It was probably very quiet when Jesus finished these stories. It was difficult for the average Jew to hear that two of their most celebrated prophets helped foreigners, while the chosen ones of Israel were suffering. Correcting a faulty premise or falsehood is never a pleasant task. Jesus was pointing a nation to the Father, who loves the whole world. God's value of humanity was on display. Sadly, those who heard this should have repented before God. But their hearts, filled with anger and hate, wanted the messenger, the prophet, killed for such words.

Validation of Scriptures and Their Dual Purpose

God incarnated came into a world to validate the Holy Spirit's words. Heresies unleashed on the Bible is a direct attack on the Holy Spirit as the author. Claims against Scripture and the writers of the Bible are mounting. Jesus quotes from Isaiah many times. On this occasion, he cites it to confront heresy.

> **John 12:38-40 –** *This was to fulfill the word of Isaiah the prophet: "Lord, who has believed our message and to whom has the arm of the Lord been revealed?" "For this reason, they could not believe, because,* **as Isaiah says elsewhere:** *he has blinded their eyes and hardened their hearts, so they can neither see with their eyes, nor understand with their hearts, nor turn—and I would heal them."*

Some question whether Isaiah was the only author of the book that bears his name, arguing it was written later or by two authors, maybe even three.

In John 12:38 Jesus quotes from **Isaiah 53:1.** Then in John 12:39, Jesus says, **"As Isaiah says elsewhere,"** and then he quotes from **Isaiah 6:10.**

Jesus citing this passage puts a hedge of protection over the entire book and the author's authenticity. In 1948, the discovery of the Dead Sea Scrolls further validated Isaiah. Isaiah was in one complete scroll. Jesus's purpose for quoting Isaiah became a double-edged sword. Addressing heretical teaching about the prophet Isaiah is oddly the side note. His main point was addressing the need to embrace the light, for he is the light. He gave them more "light" through his omniscient nature than we could realize, addressing two problems. Many prophetic Scriptures have a dual purpose, as we saw in John and Isaiah.

Even with the Dead Sea Scrolls and Jesus's affirmation of Isaiah, some theologians still try to suggest there are two authors. Could this affirm the end-time teaching of the great falling away Jesus spoke of? The Scripture addressed the unbelief of the Jews in the first century while reaching two thousand years into the future to confront our disbelief.

Ordinary people and famous people all wanted to hear what Jesus was saying—the Pharisee who visited Jesus at night seeking information about the kingdom of heaven, the Roman Centurion who wanted Jesus to touch his servant. All people want to know what he knows. Jesus, when sought, will be found. Jesus came to seek and to save the lost. He is preparing for a day when we will be with him.

The Day and Hour

Jesus affirms there will be a day and an hour when he returns. Some assume we won't know the timing but is that what he really said? His return is a two-event occasion. His second coming is when his feet land on the Mount of Olives described in Zechariah 14:4. Before his return, Jesus describes a rapture when he comes in the clouds as recorded in Luke 21:27 with power and great glory. The "Day and Hour" Jesus is referring to is the rapture and not his second coming. During his last days, Jesus prepares his apostles and us for future events. A prophetic passage can contain many time periods and events. We see this in Matthew 24.

Matthew 24

1. Jesus predicts the destruction of the temple (v. 1-2)

2. A list of futuristic events that would occur before Jesus's return (v. 4-8)

3. How society will behave toward Christians before his return (v. 9-14)

4. The sign of abomination and what Israel must do (v. 15-20)

5. A world in turmoil with increasing specific signs (v. 21-28)

6. Signs in the sun, moon, and stars (v. 29)

7. The rapture (v. 30-31)

8. Allegory of Israel and the fig tree (v. 32-34)

9. Details of how the rapture happens (v. 36-41)* Verses 30-31 connection

10. The day and the hour explained (v. 40-45)

11. The parable of the righteous and wicked behavior (v. 42-51)

Luke Chapter twenty-one gives close to the same outline, with Jesus giving us more details about the temple and signs around the rapture. There is a promise concerning the rapture that isn't in Matthew.

Luke 21:36 – *"Be always on the watch, and pray that you may be able to escape all that is about to happen and that you may be able to stand before the Son of Man."*

Watch Israel

Jesus's prophecy about the temple destruction happened almost forty years after his prophecy in 70 A.D. 1,878 years later, a prophetic watch is activated with Israel becoming a nation in 1948 A.D. There are scholars on both sides who differ on when the rapture will happen. A third camp does not believe in a rapture because the word is not used in Scripture. This group's problem is an incomplete examination of Scripture. The word Trinity is not found in Scripture, but it is an accepted concept because the entirety of Scripture bears out the existence of a Triune God. The same is true for the rapture.

Looking closer at "the day and the hour," Matthew 24:40-42 (NIV) one will be taken, and one will be left. Two men working in a field—one will be taken, and one will be left. Two women working at a mill—one will be taken, and the other will be left. The puzzle pieces only fit the rapture. One thing is for sure, Jesus did open the prophetic door. Jesus shared this during Holy Week. At the end of Jesus's natural life, he was preparing us for our next life. He was literally dying for his bride. Jesus returns for that bride and takes her to a wedding party. Jesus teaches about this event through parables.

Prophetic Parables

Parables, not often associated with prophecy, are an excellent source of God's omniscient insight. In Matthew 25 three parables are prophetic. The ten virgins, the parable of the talents, and the sheep and goats. Each has lessons about preparedness, separation, and his return. The sobering truth is **50 percent will miss out** on his return.

Matthew 25:1-13 – *Five of the ten virgins were not prepared for the bridegroom.*

Matthew 25:31-46 – *Gathering the nations and separating the people, the sheep on one side and the goats on another. The goats will end up in hell.*

In the parable of the talents (Matthew 25:14-30), a man gives his servants bags of money. To one he gives five bags, to another two bags, and to a third servant one bag—each according to their abilities. When the master returns, the servants with five bags and two bags have increased double what they received. The third servant buried his money and only returned what was given to him. Jesus said that servant was a wicked man. In addition to doing nothing with his money, he hid in his heart evil thoughts about the master. His judgment was immediate, as he was cast into hell. **One-third** of those entrusted with his possessions will suffer the consequence of poor stewardship. The agenda is not one of fear but one of preparedness and faithfulness to God. These parables were addressed to his disciples. The next parable is for the nation of Israel.

Luke 21:29-33 – *A parable of a fig tree and the events surrounding the end of time. The parable is a measurement of time comparing the fig tree blossoming with the Nation of Israel. Scholars believe the fig tree was activated when Israel as a nation was planted again like a tree in 1948. It has continued to blossom using the parable's language, regaining its capital, Jerusalem, in 1967. While bearing more traditional*

Jewish fruit, it began establishing once again a religious order.

   In August 2016, the Sanhedrin has assigned their first High priest since 70 A.D. The developing Sanhedrin was set up in Israel in 2004. It is considered a national court of Jewish Law. Over the last 500 years, there have been six failed attempts to establish a Sanhedrin. This has been the most successful attempt so far.[2]

   We need to follow Israel, their land, and their relationship to it. The key to understanding the fig tree and his second coming is connected to one special piece of property called Jerusalem.

Good Dirt

   The parable of good dirt represents a spiritually healthy heart toward God's Word. It is otherwise known as the parable of the sower and depicts how people respond to God and his Word. What is happening within their hearts and in this parable is synonymous with the ground and what's in your dirt.

   Matthew 13:1-23 – *The parable of the sower is also told in Mark 4 and Luke 8, and the details in all three give us the complete picture. The Synoptic Gospels insist on good soil for the Word to take root.*

---

[2] Dean Smith, "Jewish Sanhedrin appoints a High Priest," (September 18, 2016).

Matthew 13:23 – *If you are good soil, you hear the word and* **understand it.**

Mark 4:20 – *If you are good soil, you hear the word and* **accept it.**

Luke 8:15 – *But the seed on good soil stands for those with a noble and good heart, who hear the word,* **retain it,** *and by persevering produce a crop*[3].

Understanding the Word is not enough; accepting the Word is not going to get you there, either. The good soil represents a noble and clean heart, going beyond understanding and accepting to retaining. After persevering, your life will produce a crop. In the same manner, we must allow Jesus's

---

[3] Renee Cho, *Why Soil Matters*, April 12, 2012. Vision Share.

prophetic teachings in the parables take root in our hearts. I can hear the old farmer saying, "Don't forget, sonny, you have to start with good dirt." Another portion of this parable covers the perils of starting with unhealthy soil. Going deeper with Jesus, we stay in good soil and move into the Spirit of prophecy.

The Spirit of Prophecy

Then the angel said to me, "Write this: Blessed are those who are invited to the wedding supper of the Lamb!" And he added, "These are the true words of God." At this, I fell at his feet to worship him. But he said to me, "Don't do that! I am a fellow servant with you and with your brothers and sisters who hold to the testimony of Jesus. Worship God! For it is the Spirit of prophecy who bears testimony to Jesus."[4] John's declaration, "The Spirit of prophecy bears testimony of Jesus," elevates prophecy as the primary proof of Jesus's dual identity as the God/man. When Scripture is taken at face value and prophecy is honored, the testimony of Jesus shines. The book of Revelation is the origin of the term "Spirit of Prophecy." If we reject the concept of future prophecy still to be fulfilled, could we be accused of eliminating the words bearing the testimony of Jesus? Much of prophecy is centered on and around Jesus's life and deals with his coming into the world and his return a second time. The rejection or ridicule of prophecy is a breach or break in our relationship with the son of God. As prophecies about Jesus continue, we see him as an avenger of this prophetic passage with a graphic ending.

---

[4] Revelation 19:9-10 NIV

Kinsman Revisited

Some movies get an R rating because of graphic material. This final section of Jesus the Prophet is adult rated. When we teach children "Jesus loves me this I know, for the Bible tells us so." It's a very age-appropriate teaching. Teaching the fullness of Christ takes mature believers to realities that we don't often associate with Jesus.

We discussed kinsman redeemer in chapter two, but the tasks and obligations within the role need a little more explanation. Avenger of the blood sounds like something from a horror movie. It's the story of an ancient prophecy given hundreds of years before Jesus by the prophet Isaiah. It's called the day of vengeance. Isaiah gets graphic in describing the kinsman's garments being splattered with blood like one treading the winepress (Isaiah 63:1-4). That portrayal tethers with John's narrative of Jesus. Revelation 19:13-15 – "He is dressed in a robe dipped in blood, and his name is the Word of God. The armies of heaven were following him, riding on white horses and dressed in fine linen, white and clean. Coming out of his mouth is a sharp sword with which to strike down the nations. 'He will rule them with an iron scepter.' He treads the winepress of the fury of the wrath of God Almighty."

For many years, I associated Jesus's robe dipped in blood with our salvation. One day reading an account in the Old Testament alerted me to the prophecy of Jesus's robe being covered in the blood of the enemies of God. Isaiah 63:2-3 – "Why are your garments red, like those of one treading the winepress? 'I have trodden the winepress alone; from the nations, no one was with me. I trampled them in my anger and trod them down in my wrath; their blood spattered my garments, and I stained all my clothing.'

What an entirely different perspective we receive when we know the origin of Scripture. The fulfillment of Scripture is observed through the lens of the past as well as future events. Saints and martyrs of faith are waiting for the fulfillment of this prophecy. Jesus is a returning warrior who comes to fulfill this day of reckoning. It's known as the day of vengeance of our Lord. His role is the Kinsman Redeemer who avenges the blood. God is taking vengeance as he promised us. He would do so in order that revenge would not be our agenda. For vengeance is mine saith the Lord.[5]

Guardrails give us clues which enhance our ability in the interpretation of God's Word when it comes to prophecy. Remember the picture you're seeing is not a blurry one, but one of the fullness of God. It is a view of the Holy God you've trusted. He is showing his calling card or ID and all the other facets of who he is. The operating mode is a futuristic one until it's accomplished. Looking deeply into God's omniscient power provides confidence in his sovereignty. Because God knows everything, only he can keep himself accountable.

---

[5] Romans 12:19 NIV

CHAPTER 4

Guardrails for Prophetic
Scripture

Proverbs 22:28
*Do not move an ancient boundary stone set up by
your ancestors. (NIV)*

On February 13, 1975, Carl Baker and I became best friends while attending college in Colorado Springs. On a trip to speak at a youth rally, we needed a guardrail to save our lives. There wasn't a human guardrail built on that point of the mountain called Wolf Creek Pass where our car hit the ice. God provided the nice soft railing called a snowbank, and we are here today to tell the story because a God-made barrier prevented us from falling to our deaths.

Guardrails are placed on the road to keep you from going into an unsafe area. They are positioned as a boundary and a warning. If you hit the rail, you will have some damage to your car, but you will still be ok. Guardrails are a source of protection but cannot stop a speeding car where the person is determined to pass them.

There are ancient boundaries! The borders of biblical truth must not be violated. What happens when Christians don't see parameters in God's Word? They go outside of those margins. They will break with the instructions and boundaries of God's Word. In doing so, they lose their protection. There are healthy guidelines for marriage, love, and all relationships. The all-knowing God uses prophetic Scriptures as warnings and as opportunities to prepare us. They can also be a guardrail. We are, sadly, not preparing for the coming wrath of God; instead, we are still trying to decide if we can trust the Scriptures.

It's time for an educated and open discussion on the inerrancy of Scripture. In some cases, I have heard members of academia brag that they have never preached on prophecy. Others have proudly proclaimed that they will not preach from the first eleven chapters of the Bible. The next generation is being taught only the historical view of Genesis and Revelation. I believe every Christian should be equipped with the knowledge of prophetic Scriptures. Believing the clues and understanding them will draw you to God. Every time I read a prophetic passage, my concept of God gets expanded. However, teaching a limited historical perspective shrinks the Bible and God to something less than eternal. We need the guardians of the faith who pass this knowledge from generation to generation to stand firm on the Word of God.

Guardrail Protection #1
Prophecy is not something God invented. It reveals the all-knowing God.

If we make prophecy anything other than the revealing of God's omniscient power, we are guilty of misrepresenting God.

No church, person, or religious organization invented prophecy. It has always been the number one-way God reveals himself as God because only he is omniscient. The Gospels reinforced this truth in several ways. Luke and Mark both observe Jesus's omniscience in knowing what people were thinking about the person with paralysis and his response to the man's need.

Luke 5:22 (NIV) – *Jesus* **knew what they were thinking** *and asked, "Why are you thinking these things in your hearts?"*

Mark 2:8 (NIV) – *Immediately,* **Jesus knew in his spirit that this was what they were thinking** *in their hearts, and he said to them, "Why are you thinking these things?"*

Matthew 9:4 (NIV) – *Knowing their thoughts, Jesus said,* **"Why do you entertain evil thoughts** *in your hearts?"*

In Matthew's version of the paralytic, Jesus identifies a deeper, darker side of people. Jesus knows our hearts and even our motivations. The crowd's heart issue is revealed when Jesus said to the paralytic your sins are forgiven. The act of forgiveness exposed contempt in their heart and their unbelief about Jesus.

Three gospel writers draw attention to Jesus's omniscient power in the story. When seeing reliable verification of a passage by multiple biblical witnesses, a question comes to mind. Did this event fulfill a prophecy Jeremiah gave concerning Jesus? Jeremiah 20:12 (NIV) – "Yet O LORD of hosts, you who test the righteous, who see the mind and the heart; Let me see Your vengeance on them; For to You I have set forth my cause."

The cherry on the top is the fulfillment of Jeremiah's prophecy. The paralyzed man's healing is paramount for the individual. Also, the prophetic fulfillment for the masses is critical information. The man going home forgiven for his sins and walking is priceless.

The evidence is Jesus connects with his father's character.

1. **Omniscience:** Jesus knows what the crowds were thinking. Only God can do this.
2. **Holiness:** Jesus has the power to forgive sins. Only God can do this.
3. **Omnipotent:** He sends the man home, hop skipping down the road (my interpretation). Again, only God can do this.

The power to see the mind and heart is reserved for God alone. Here's a comforting truth, the devil or others can't read our minds or our hearts. The above attributes are establishing the groundwork for how different God is from anyone. A one-dimensional god is not our God. If you only view God through the lens of one trait, you've created your god. A dangerous pattern is developing, people giving God the single overriding attribute of love. God's love cannot take away from him being "Just." Doing so diminishes the totality of him as the supreme being. Through prophecy, we learn about God's love, mercy, justice, power, presence, and wrath. The prophetic Scriptures reveal the whole sum of God's attributes.

Guardrail Protection #2
Prophetic Scripture can have multiple time periods; therefore, they have a split fulfillment.

> **Isaiah 9:6 (NIV)** – *"For to us a child is born, to us a son is given, and the government will be on his shoulders. And he will be called Wonderful Counselor, Mighty God, Everlasting Father, Prince of Peace."*

In this verse, we see two prophecies and timelines. The first period is detailing Jesus's birth. The second applies to his reign from David's throne. The latter event has not yet happened; it is predicted to occur during the millennium reign of Jesus. Multiple time periods and their fulfillment within a passage is one clue that it is prophetic. The reading gets a new set of eyes when viewing prophetic Scripture. Jesus's teaching on end times in the Olivet discourse raises the question of time periods. You should always ask questions about what period is being addressed. It's not unusual for some passages to have several time periods. We see this often in the book of Isaiah. Reading the text without this kind of insight, the reader reverts to looking at Scripture through a historical lens and misses the deeper meaning. Here's an example to develop your spiritual eyesight.

> **Matthew 20:18-19 (NIV)** – *"We are going up to Jerusalem, and the Son of Man will be delivered over to the chief priests and the teachers of the law. They will condemn him to death and will hand him over to the Gentiles to be*

*mocked and flogged and crucified. On the third day, he will
be raised to life!"*

Before they go to Jerusalem and experience the triumphal
entry known as Palm Sunday, he gives them this prophecy. It
is a clear prophecy that shows future events in the exact order it
happens. We wish all such prophecies were so easy to identify,
but not all puzzles are easy. Think of this passage as a template to
see more details in prophetic statements.

1. The mocking at the trial and public rejection
2. The flogging of Jesus and his crucifixion
3. The resurrection three days later

These prophetic insights gives the ability to preach about the
garden of Gethsemane with renewed passion. Why? I know
what Jesus knows going into the garden because of this prophetic
passage.

This example doesn't have the length between each event
as Isaiah 9:6, but you can see it's not a hard task for God to give
several events and time periods in illuminating the future through
Scriptures.

Guardrail Protection #3
**Scriptures directed to an unsaved Israel prophetically don't
apply them to a saved church.**

Specific Scriptures are warnings or insights for Israel's future.
As a nation throughout the Old Testament, they had a wayward

relationship with God. Replacement theology is taking a portion of Scripture directed toward Israel and applying it to the church. Replacement theology is bad theology and poor interpretation. The church is not God's plan B for the world. God has never given up on Israel and will redeem them.

> **Isaiah 54:5-6 (NIV)** – *"For your Maker is your husband— the LORD Almighty is his name—the Holy One of Israel is your Redeemer; he is called the God of all the earth. The LORD will call you back as if you were a wife deserted and distressed in spirit—a wife who married young, only to be rejected,' says your God."*

God has a specific purpose and a plan for the nation of Israel. He also has a unique role and plan for the church as well. He has a plan for your life. Learning about your blueprint and purpose starts when you invite Jesus into our heart.

> **Ephesians 3:9-11 (NIV)** – *"And to make plain to everyone the administration of this mystery, which for ages past was kept hidden in God, who created all things. His intent was that now,* **through the church, the manifold wisdom of God should be made known to the rulers** *and authorities in the heavenly realms, according to his eternal purpose that he accomplished in Christ Jesus our Lord."*

The church has a unique assignment in the world. It's different from Israel. This becomes more evident as we understand the prophetic role of Israel. The wisdom to comprehend their future is hidden because of their rejection of Jesus. The knowledge has been given to the church, and it's our role to prepare Israel and the world for the future.

The make-up of the body of Christ does include Jews—Messianic Jews. Many have accepted Jesus. There has been an accelerated pace of Jews receiving Jesus since the recapture of Jerusalem in 1967. More Jews are coming to Jesus Christ and accepting him as their Messiah than even in the first-century church. This could be the signal that the Gentile's time is coming to an end. A shift and focus are on Israel once again as the center of the world. Luke 21:24 (NIV) – They will fall by the sword and will be taken as prisoners to all the nations. Jerusalem will be trampled on by the Gentiles until the times of the Gentiles are fulfilled.

This points to the end of the church age, which signals the rapture could be close. The book of Revelation is written with Israel in mind. Scholars have noted that after Chapter 4 of Revelation, the church is in the background. Judgment, the redemption of the world, and Israel are significant themes in Revelation.

Guardrail Protection #4
Look for Prophecy within patterns or typology.

Old Testament prophets who were less than 100 percent correct were false prophets. It was grounds to be put to death. A job description with this advertisement should keep people from wanting to identify as a prophet. I know it puts the fear of the Lord into my soul. Scholars validate the accuracy of prophetic books like Daniel and Isaiah. We conclude Bible prophecies must be accurate, including the rapture, the millennium, the judgment, and eternity. These subjects bring us to a substantial introduction, to biblical patterns, shadows, and cycles. My Rabbi friend, the late Herb Opalek, held two doctorates, was my source to what he called Hebrew patterns. Accuracy is essential when matching types and shadows. The Scripture recognizes types and shadows on many subjects. The best example is Jesus. His comparison to several Old Testament figures will become apparent.

Types or Shadows in Scripture

In the Old Testament, patterns or typology is prophecy. It's a prediction of another kind. Throughout the Bible, there are prototypes, or patterns, or figures of things to come. They give the structure of an unfolding event.

According to the writer of Hebrews, Jesus is considered a priest in the order of Melchizedek because, like Melchizedek, Jesus was not a descendant of Aaron and, thus, would not qualify for the Jewish priesthood under the Law of Moses.[1]

> **Hebrews 7:1-3 (NIV)** – *"For this Melchizedek, king of Salem, priest of the Most-High God, who met Abraham as he was returning from the slaughter of the kings and blessed him, to whom also Abraham apportioned a tenth part of all the spoils, was first, by the translation of his name, king of righteousness, and then also king of Salem, which is king of peace. Without father, without mother, without genealogy,*

---

[1] https://en.wikipedia.org/wiki/Melchizedek

*having neither beginning of days nor end of life, but made
like the Son of God, he remains a priest perpetually."*

Abraham gives a tithe to Melchizedek, the Old Testament
King of Salem and a High Priest. See, Genesis 14:18-19. This
creates the scenarios of the two offices of King and High Priest
as a "Type or Shadow." The identification of Jesus in the order of
Melchizedek highlights the two roles of Jesus. It also highlights
his reason for coming, as well as a prophetic message to the
world—one to be king and second to be the High priest. The
High priest in the Jewish culture is required to sacrifice once
a year for the sins of all the people. Jesus became the sacrifice
once and for all. Remember, prophetic Scripture must be 100
percent true. If Jesus was only a King and not our High priest,
then this Scripture could not be applied to him. There is a little
twist to the story affirming Melchizedek as a typecast of Jesus.
Melchizedek was King of Salem, the old Hebrew name for the
city of Jerusalem. Scripture declares Jesus will rule from Jerusalem
during his second coming to earth (Isaiah 9:6-7, 17) At this point,
Jesus has fulfilled two of three foreshadows of his reign in Isaiah.

1. He was born King of the Jews.
2. As High Priest, he became the sacrifice for humanity.
3. His ruling from David's throne in Jerusalem is still
    a future event.

His return is the only way to make this typology of a
prophetic Scripture 100% accurate.

Guardrail Protection #5

Prophetic Scriptures can have a natural and literal interpretation and should be viewed through that lens first unless symbolism is apparent.

> **David L. Cooper's golden rule states,** *"When the plain sense of the Scripture makes sense, seek no other sense."*[2]

I read Perry Stone, Hal Lindsey, Jonathan Cahn, Chuck Missler, and others outside of the Wesleyan movement to get a fuller perspective. They add a brick or two in making a case for sound doctrine on God's will and omniscient power. Total reliance on any one author or theologian is irresponsible. We must all be students of Scripture, correctly handling the word of truth is everyone's responsibility.

Which Scriptures should fall into the classification of allegory? Can Scriptures be taken literally? Some have even suggested that Adam and Eve are an allegory for humanity. Making such a stance is ignoring biblical evidence within the Genealogies. Genesis, Matthew, and Luke place them alongside their descendants. It seems crazy to have to mention such a fact, but this is how farfetched some of our schools have gone in their scholastics.

> **Psalm 119:105 (NIV)** – *Your word is a lamp for my feet, a light on my path.*

When teaching prophecy in the early 1990s, my presentations were weighted toward allegory. I referred to the martyr saints

---

[2] David L Cooper, "The Golden Rule of Interpretation," 47.

having been beheaded and standing before the throne of God asking, "When will we be avenged?"[3] With confidence, I gave assurances that in the 20th century, our world won't stand for such a thing. The uncivilized behavior mentioned was only pointing to them as martyrs of the faith. Well, the world isn't civilized, and literally tens of thousands of saints have been beheaded. The longer I study the Scripture, a more literal meaning is becoming evident.

The Bible is not a document trying to trick us. Stories that are parables are stated as such. Proverbs and the poetic sections address such categories. Symbols, when used, interpret themselves. Often the clue to a symbol is found in other parts of the Bible, such as Joseph's dream in Genesis about the twelve stars, the sun, and the moon bowing down to him. Jacob has no problem figuring out the message and is astonished by this dream. Jacob asked, "Will even your mother and I bow down to you along with your brothers?" Jacob knew exactly what the dream was saying. You recognize more biblical symbols than you think. If people with biblical knowledge hear the word serpent or dragon, they reason it's Satan. Say the word dove, and we think of the Holy Spirit. The word lamb immediately suggests Jesus. The Scripture is the best tool to figure out Scripture even regarding symbols.

Guardrail Protection #6
Scripture interprets Scripture.

> **Hebrews 4:12 (NIV)** – *For the word of God is alive and active. Sharper than any double-edged sword, it penetrates*

---

3   Revelation 20:4 NIV

even to dividing soul and spirit, joints and marrow; it judges the thoughts and attitudes of the heart.

Scripture is the trump card. In our Wesleyan tradition, we call Scripture the seat of the stool. The legs are Church history, reason, experience, and culture are additional supports. All play a role in interpretation. The legs never trump or remove the seat. Scripture is supreme. Hermeneutics is vital to our endeavor to have a sound biblical interpretation. Keeping Scripture in the supreme position is never a risk. Jesus said, "Let no one deceive you." In the last days, the hearts of many will grow cold.[4] The implication is there was a time when their hearts were hot for the truth. Threats of deception come from everywhere, but the risk from within is the most dangerous. If we are blind guides, how can we lead the blind? Those who have an ear to hear, listen to the insight of Paul. "All Scripture is God-breathed and is useful for **teaching, rebuking, correcting and training** in righteousness, so that the servant of God may be thoroughly equipped for every good work." All Scripture is from God and useful for training.[5] The four directives are our tools, and they will enhance your life and equip you for good works.

The Word of God has faced more perplexing attacks in the last twenty years than it has in the previous two thousand years. Did it start by changing the stance on Bible inerrancy? Jesus, along with Paul and Isaiah, declares the Word of God will last forever. Do you think God wants a flawed book to be around

---

[4] Matthew 24:12 NIV

[5] 2 Timothy 3:16-17 NIV

forever—a reminder that the all-powerful God allowed mistakes to get into his Holy Bible? Could the perceived errors be only the limitation of human knowledge?

We don't deny the Hermeneutics of history, culture, and experience. But we must not allow them to override the seat of power in the Scripture themselves.

> **Isaiah 55:10-11 (NIV)** – *"As the rain and the snow come down from heaven, and do not return to it without watering the earth and making it bud and flourish, so that it yields seed for the sower and bread for the eater, so is my word that goes out from my mouth: It will not return to me empty, but will accomplish what I desire and achieve the purpose for which I sent it."*

A prophecy within a prophetic Scripture is taking place in Isaiah 55:11. These are powerful words from God's heart about his Word never being empty or returning void. The emphasis is on the Word of God accomplishing what God desires it to achieve. If you are a preacher, your hearers don't need to know what books you've been reading. They need to hear the Word of God proclaimed with confidence. Paraphrasing Isaiah, in this prophetic passage, his promises are not cheap empty words; they are the words of life. Once they are inside you, they will anchor your soul for all eternity.

CHAPTER 5

Mysteries within the Jewish Feasts/Festivals

J esus grew up observing all the feasts/festivals; these two words are interchangeable. What if everything about the Jewish people, their customs, and their feasts was given to them by God to point to one person? Could their feasts/festivals all have to do with the carpenter's son, Jesus of Nazareth? To explore this truth, we must once again go to the beginning of Genesis. Laying down a proper understanding of the sacred will help connect the pieces to the sacred one.

After Adam and Eve sinned, God divulged his plan. One day, a woman's seed would defeat the devil. Pointing to Jesus, his life will bring restoration for all humanity. God chooses a people and land to work out the details. The people will be the Jews, and the land is Israel. The father of the Jews won't be born for two thousand years. It takes an additional two thousand years for the seed to be planted into a virgin. God is never in a rush, for the journey is just as important as the destination.

Back on the fourth day of creation, he prophesied about the sacred. He created holy days for the Jews and the land. They serve as seven key pieces to our puzzle. The pathway to the sacred and a holy life will be through their trials and tribulations.

> **Genesis 1:14** – *"And God said, 'Let there be lights in the vault of the sky to separate the day from the night and let them serve as signs to mark sacred times, and days and years.'*

After years of studying the seven feasts, I believe the value of observing the Jewish feasts goes beyond Israel. The study is as relevant, if not more in some ways, for our society and beliefs than for the Jews themselves.

The feasts could prove to be vital for the millennial and generation Z. Both have had so little in the way of traditions or absolutes. This knowledge of the holy or sacred times was tucked into our world as a connector to the eternal truth. This merging culture must discover the feast as an anchor in their ever-changing world. I am not suggesting they must participate in the festivals. But I am passionately proposing that the teaching of the feasts will open the door to new spiritual dimensions. Connecting to the events, times, and mysteries in God's Word will help us attach to God and the world in a new, relevant way.

We are introduced to the seven feasts within the trials and adventures of the nation of Israel as they came out of captivity and into the promised land God had given them. The Jewish journey becomes a reminder of God's intervention every step of the way. Secrets for the Jew as well as for the believer are found in their sacred days and the seven mysteries.

God lives outside of time in eternity and can look at life through that eternal lens. God did this while creating and marking sacred times, days, and years.

Leviticus 23:2 – *"Speak to the Israelites and say to them: 'These are my appointed festivals, the appointed festivals of the LORD, which you are to proclaim as sacred assemblies."*

God sets within these days the purpose of consecration, holiness, and a pattern through the secrecies of the feasts.

"The scared times *could be the true meaning of* Jewish holiness. *The Hebrew word for holiness, kedushah, literally means set aside, designated as different." The obligations to sanctify space and time are woven together, Says Rabbi Kukla.*[1]

Any time set aside for God is a sacred time. The context of Genesis 1:14 is God marking the sacred times with the creation of the sun, moon, and stars. God sets aside a day from our routine for rest and extra time with him. This simple pattern is known to us as the Sabbath day. A holy day to worship and to experience a spiritual community with those who gather for a time set aside for the sacred. Those elements motivate my heart to make sure our Sundays have these ingredients. Nothing will attract the lost more than something they can't have anywhere else. The first feast is known as Passover, and it came at a time filled with unrest and uncertainty.

---

[1] Rabbi Kukla, "Sacred Time and Space."

The Jewish calendar is rooted in the cycles of the moon. Each month of the year is a lunar month, beginning on the new moon and ending when the moon is dark. [2]

Passover

February 3, 2018 marks the first birthday of my fifth grandchild, Paisley Marie. While she was in her mother's womb, the Passover story became alive for me. Hannah developed five life-threating blood clots during her pregnancy. When the doctor informed us she and the baby were at risk, I sought God on how we should pray for her during this time. He drew me to pray the blood of our Savior, the Lamb of God, over Hannah and Paisley's lives every day. It has become a practice that I continue not just for them, but now for my whole household, all my children's marriages, and grandchildren.

After four hundred years, slavery in Israel was a way of life. The Egyptian Empire ruled them for exactly four hundred years. No generations alive could remember freedom. The story takes place the night before everything changes and they are released from their captivity. Egypt had experienced nine supernatural plagues by the hand of God, who just disclosed the tenth plague to Moses. The Jewish people were instructed on this night the need for a quick meal. Because in the morning, everything must be packed and ready to go. God will make this rushed meal one they will never forget. A meal would be practiced and relived for all Jewish generations to come because that night there was more than packing and a quick dinner. It would be a night of judgment.

---

[2] Jill Hammer, "Jewish Cycles of the Moon."

Passover is a seven-day feast. They were instructed to kill a lamb, take its blood, and mark their doors. Exodus 12:13 – "The blood shall be a sign for you, on the houses where you are. And when I see the blood, I will pass over you, and no plague will befall you to destroy you, when I strike the land of Egypt."

It seems like an eerie, weird thing to do, but hidden within this symbolic act is a prophecy filled with hope and future for the whole world. Initially, the command was that no foreigner was to eat the Passover meal. It was only for Israel. After Jesus, the Lamb of God was slain on Calvary, we are all invited to the table of remembrance. That blood opens the door for all to break free from their captivity of sin just as Israel would break free from their slavery. We had no original part in Passover, and because of sin, we were under a death sentence. Death now can pass over our lives when the Lamb's blood is applied to the doorway of our hearts. It's the blood of the spotless lamb of God (Jesus) that gives us a claim to holiness. God's patterns are used again and again, showing there is a double meaning behind the fulfillment of the Jewish feasts. Before the seven days of Passover are completed, we share in two more festivals. The Jewish customs and traditions reveal a complete portrait of the redemption for the whole world.

The Feast of Unleavened Bread

My wife Mindy loves going to someone's home, especially if they are making bread or any baked goods. So for everyone like Mindy, here's the recipe for making unleavened bread. Why not make some for Easter celebration and tell the Passover story to your family?

Mix flour, oil, and salt together in a bowl; add water and mix using a pastry cutter until dough is soft. Form dough into 6 balls and press into disks onto the prepared baking sheet using your hands. Bake in the preheated oven until **bread** *is cooked, 8 to 10 minutes.*[3]

Remember this day in which you came out from Egypt, out of the house of slavery, for by a strong hand the Lord brought you out from this place. No leavened bread shall be eaten.[4] There is a hidden meaning behind bread that has no yeast. Yeast was a symbol to the Jewish people for sin. Jesus uses this knowledge to teach the kingdom of God. "Knowing that a little yeast will work through a whole dough of bread, as a little sin will work through a whole person's life."[5]

Jesus also declares he is the Bread of Life. He is the fulfillment of the Feast of Unleavened Bread. The little twist to the analogy is the reminder. He alone can deliver us from the slavery of sin. You cannot leave out the irony of while in the wilderness for forty years, God was the delivery man or bread man with his daily supply of food, bread from Heaven.

Clues Pointing to a Savior

1. Jesus is the real bread of heaven.
2. Jesus came declaring he is the Bread of Life. Like manna, he came from heaven.

---

[3] allrecipes.com/recipe/241680/unleavened-bread-for-communion/

[4] Exodus 13:3 NIV

[5] Matthew 13:33 NIV

3.   He was unleavened bread, for he knew no sin.

The feast patterns develop, the story within the story now moves from bread to fruit.

The Feast of Firstfruits

Everyone loves fruit when it is in season. I can still hear the cart being pushed down the streets of my neighborhood. The street vendor singing out, "Bananas, blueberries, and strawberries." There is something about the smell of fresh fruit. This brings us to the third feast, yet we are still within the time-period of the first feast of Passover. This feast occurs the day after the Feast of Unleavened Bread. There is nothing as magical as the first harvest of the year.

> **Leviticus 23:10 (NIV)** – *"Speak to the Israelites and say to them: 'When you enter the land I am going to give you and you reap its harvest, bring to the priest a sheaf of the first grain you harvest."*

The Feast of Firstfruits was not initiated until the Israelites entered the promised land. This was an offering to remind Israel that God keeps his promises. It's also a very popular Christian's holiday. When the pieces of this feast connect to Jesus's life, we have our highest holy day in Christianity—Easter! But Christ has indeed been raised from the dead, **the firstfruits** of those who have fallen asleep.[6]

You've heard the phrase, "Timing is everything?" Watch the sequence of the puzzle coming together.

---

[6]   I Corinthians 15:20 NIV

1. **Feast of Passover:** Jesus becomes the Passover Lamb whose blood marks our lives.

2. **Feast of Unleavened Bread:** Jesus becomes the Bread of Life, and when we eat of this bread, we live.

3. **Feast of Firstfruits:** Jesus is raised from the dead on this day. We celebrate the resurrection.

Jesus's half-brother, James, writes in the book of James about our role in God's plan. He gives us the puzzle behind the Feast of Firstfruits Celebration. "He chose to give us birth through the word of truth that we might be a kind of firstfruits of all he created."[7]

The ripple effect happens as every Christian experiences a celebrated resurrected life. All of heaven celebrated you accepting Jesus. To make sure we have the power to live this kind of life, we have our next feast, Pentecost.

The Feast of Pentecost

There is a waiting period between the first three feasts and the fourth one. What was happening on earth with Jesus's disciples? They were waiting in an upper room after the death and resurrection of Jesus. They had spent several weeks with him since those events. They even watched him ascend to heaven. Now they were waiting on the promise of receiving the Holy Spirit. They were in an upper room praying on the first day of

---

[7] James 1:18 NIV

the week, Sunday. They knew it was also the Feast of Pentecost. They had gone to honor this time, commemorating the giving of the Law to Moses while they were in the wilderness.

> **Leviticus 23:15 (NIV)** – *"From the day after the Sabbath, the day you brought the sheaf of the wave offering, count off seven full weeks. Count off fifty days up to the day after the seventh Sabbath, and then present an offering of new grain to the LORD."*

Pentecost means fifty; some Jews call it the mini jubilee they celebrate each year. It's known also as "The Feast of the Weeks." Its name came about because of the counting of seven weeks from the Feast of Firstfruits.

The Birth of the church is on this same day as the outpouring of the Holy Spirit on Pentecost. I love birthday celebrations, and this feast is one of my favorites. – "When the day of Pentecost came, they were all together in one place. Suddenly, a sound like the blowing of a violent wind came from heaven and filled the whole house where they were sitting. They saw what seemed to be tongues of fire that separated and came to rest on each of them. All of them were filled with the Holy Spirit and began to speak in other tongues as the Spirit enabled them. Now there were staying in Jerusalem God-fearing Jews from every nation under heaven. When they heard this sound, a crowd came together in bewilderment, because each one heard their own language being spoken. Utterly amazed, they asked: 'Aren't all these who are speaking Galileans? Then how is it that each of us hears them in our native language?'[8]

---

[8] Acts 2:1-8 NIV

When the Holy Spirit came on Pentecost, he continued the string of double fulfillment in our Jewish feasts, once again enlarging the purpose of these feast for humanity. Some scholars who study end times even wonder if there is another future fulfillment of the Feast of Pentecost? But for now, the feast cycle goes through a whole summer without any activity. But, oh, the fall period is a busy feast/festival season. It starts with a blast, a trumpet blast that is.

The Feast of Trumpets

The fifth through seventh feasts all take place in the seventh month called Tishri. Besides announcing the introduction to the seventh month, it also signals the final cycle of the feast/festival season. The Trumpets feast is one of the more unique celebrations, as it's a memorial to all that has taken place before any feast/festival. It is a time of remembrance.

> **Leviticus 23:24 (NIV)** – *"Say to the Israelites: 'On the first day of the seventh month you are to have a day of Sabbath rest, a sacred assembly commemorated with trumpet blasts.'*

It also signals the end of the harvest season and the beginning of 10 days of consecration of the New Year. There will be 90 blasts of the trumpet in a two-day period, followed by a time called the seven days of affliction or seven terrible days. Are the three fall feasts linked to Jesus in the same manner the first four spring feasts are tied to him? Eschatologists have always had a special relationship with the Feast of Trumpets because of the firm long-term belief that Jesus would come for his Church in the rapture during this feast. "At the trumpet sound the dead in Christ will rise first, and we who are still alive will be caught up with them." Paul's letter to the Thessalonians has become the cornerstone of this belief and makes this one of the most popular views of this feast. There are several reasons why it might not be about the rapture but have some other futuristic fulfillment. "You also must be ready, because the Son of Man will come at an hour when you do not expect him."[9] But about that day or hour no one knows, not even the angels in heaven, nor the Son, but only the Father.[10]

When Jesus says we cannot know the day or the hour of his return, Jews believed he was pointing to the Feast of Trumpets. It, too, was known as the feast that no man knows the day or hour. It takes two Jewish witnesses going to the High Priest and declaring they saw the new moon. Then, the order is given to blow the shofar, commencing this first of the fall feast/festival.

Again, my desire is not to set dates on such things but to enlighten us on the potential of these Scriptures' fulfillment. Some scholars suggest the first four feasts are linked to the church, while the last three feasts/festivals may be connected to Israel. We can only wait and see, for to say anything else would be a guess. It could be an educated guess, but no real prophet risks God's wrath on such a thing.

---

[9] Luke 12:40 NIV

[10] Matthew 24:36 NIV

The Day of Atonement

This feast draws me back to my Catholic Church experiences. Catholics have a lot of worship practices in the style of Jewish temple worship.

1. The need for a man to give absolution of the sin for others. (This is the Jewish High Priest's role.)

2. Certain parts of the church are off limits to regular people. (Only the Jewish priest has access to the temple area called the Holy of Holies.)

3. Salvation comes through the ritual of the ongoing sacrifice. Communion is offered in every mass. (The Jewish High Priest must offer a sacrifice each year on behalf of the whole nation.)

The Scripture instructs us to take communion in remembrance of what was done on our behalf. The Protestant Church sees salvation as an act done once for all, Jesus dying on the cross. We honor the remembrance of the deed through communion.

There are some wonderful resources online about the feast. Here is one.

Described in Leviticus 16:1-34, the atonement ritual began with Aaron, or subsequent high priests of Israel, coming into the holy of holies. The solemnity of the day was underscored by God telling Moses to warn Aaron not to come into the Most Holy Place whenever he felt like it, only on this special day once a year, lest he die (v. 2). This was not a ceremony to be taken lightly, and **the people were to understand that atonement for sin was to be done God's way.** *Before entering the tabernacle, Aaron was to bathe and put on special garments (v. 4), then sacrifice a bull for a sin offering for himself and his family (v. 6, 11). The blood of the bull was to be sprinkled on the ark of the covenant. Then Aaron was to bring two goats, one to be sacrificed "because of the uncleanness and rebellion of the Israelites, whatever their sins have been" (v. 16), and its blood was sprinkled on the ark of the covenant. The other goat was used as a scapegoat. Aaron placed his hands on its head, confessed over it the rebellion and wickedness of the Israelites, and sent the goat out with an appointed man who released it into the wilderness (v. 21). The goat carried on itself all the sins of the people, which were forgiven for another year (v. 30).*[11]

The most interesting new fact about The Day of Atonement is on August 29, 2016, the Sanhedrin appointed *Rabbi Baruch Kahane as High Priest*[12]. *He* rejected it the next day. But this shows the readiness of the Sanhedrin to reestablish the temple sacrifices. You can follow this ongoing process by googling "Temple Institute." This is in anticipation of being able to fulfill their obligation to their nation someday soon. The priests in Israel have been waiting to honor the Day of Atonement on behalf of the nation of Israel—a feat that has not been accomplished since 70 A.D.

---

[11] "On the day of atonement," Got Questions.org.

[12] "Sanhedrin Appoints High Priest in Preparation for Third Temple," Breakingnewsisrael.com.

The connection of the Day of Atonement and Jesus are throughout the Scriptures. As discussed in Chapter two, only one person can make the atonement for the people—the High Priest. Jesus is declared High Priest in the order of Melchizedek (Hebrews 5:10). Within this Scripture is the fact that he must be a spotless High Priest. Israel still waits for this prophecy to be fulfilled. They have *not as a nation* recognized Jesus as the fulfillment of the Messiah. The ceremonial ritual of purification to cleanse the high priest of any sin must be followed. If there were hidden sins in a priest's life, he would die in the presence of the Holy God. Therefore, they would tie a long cord around the high priest's ankle when he went into the Holy of Holies to retrieve him in case he died. There is a great message every Christian should read about atonement. "The Day of Atonement" by the Famous Charles Spurgeon number 95 August 10, 1856.

The Scapegoat

In modern terms, a scapegoat is a person who takes the blame for the wrongdoing of others. In the act of atonement, they kill one goat for the sins of the nation while setting another one free. The scapegoat is the one put to death so the other may live. The incredible parallel is powerful. This is a prophetic picture of Jesus representing humanity or, in this instance, the innocent goat that is slain. Jesus willingly dies for the sins of the world while we are set free. Imagine what kind of gift this is. We were the wrongdoers, the guilty ones, and he took our place. Also, he offers us life everlasting with him in heaven. This is a beautiful picture of our part of the puzzle, but is there a role for the day of atonement still in Israel's future? Absolutely.

The Feast of Tabernacles

In the summer of 1969, my mother and a neighboring mother took eleven children camping in a park alongside the Chesapeake Bay. Sleeping out in tents is much more fun when you're young. You lay there in your sleeping bag looking up while telling stories to each other. Well, welcome to the Feast of Tabernacles. This happens every year for families who still build tents, but it's more like a teepee because of the hole in the roof. They lay there telling the ancient stories of family ancestors wandering in the wilderness.

The events are known by different names in Jewish culture. Sukkot or Succot, literally Feast of Booths, is commonly translated into English as **Feast of Tabernacles**, sometimes also as Feast of the Ingathering. This feast/festival is the seventh of all the feasts and is also one of the three major feasts. It's the only one in Scriptures celebrated in Jesus's future thousand-year reign on the earth—the period called the millennium. Why would this feast get such a high honor? Could this be the feast that marks the second coming of Jesus? It has in it beautiful imagery of the preparation of a wedding. There are the rituals of praise and reenactments to God's faithfulness for providing water in the desert for forty consecutive years. Specific prayers are repeated during the seven nights, staring up at the stars. The anticipation is something great will happen. The parents tell the children that the God of creation could magically appear. They have kept the hope of this becoming a reality alive for four thousand years. Each generation is wondering if it will be their privilege to be invited to the wedding party with the Bridegroom of Creation.

The Feast of Tabernacles lasts for seven days. There is a specific honor given to God for taking care of them while in the wilderness—the water they drank and the manna they ate. Like the Feast of Trumpets, it's a time of remembrance, honoring a God who sustained their people for forty years. Their history says their clothes didn't even wear out. I believe that's supernatural. It makes me wonder how the ladies reacted who experienced the miracle of the everlasting wardrobe. The negative could have gone like this, "I've been wearing the same thing for the last forty years." While the positive could have gone like this, "I still fit in my same clothes after forty years." Either way, it points to God being able to take care of them whatever their needs were. The feast/festivals are complete, but not our eternal hook-up with the Jewish people or with the sacredness of God.

Judeo-Christian

When my mom went shopping, she never went for a few items. Eight hungry mouths were waiting at home to be fed. She made sure she had plenty of what we called staples on hand. The seven feast/festivals are the staples of the Jewish tradition. The Jewish sacred days help bond important holy pieces to the Christian faith puzzle. There are articles of faith in each Judeo-Christian season that point to God's plan and purposes. The feast is where the list begins. The objective is to take us on a journey through Scriptures to a bigger picture. One that will anchor your soul as nothing else can.

Using the Jewish/Christian insights to the feasts will give your ministry a new urgency when preaching. For example, on resurrection day, you can guide your congregation in the background to the Feasts of Passover, Unleavened Bread, and Firstfruits. Teaching on the Holy Spirit and the many fulfillments of the Feast of Pentecost should ignite new excitement about the Holy Spirit and his role in the last days. Many of my eschatology friends believe the church's birth on Pentecost would be a high watch season. The groom might choose to come and sweep away his bride as a birthday surprise? Yes, that's speculation, but it's possible. Any feast could link with his return.

No Obligation

God is not obligated to send his Son to any feast or during any particular time on the Jewish calendar. Jesus's promise is that he will return, and that's all we need to know. There is an old doctrine called the doctrine of imminence. When Jesus ascended into heaven, the angel spoke these words: "In the same manner you saw him go, he will return." The disciples believed they would see his return in their time. Every generation has lived with the hope of his return. We can study the prophecies and see the paper trail in all the feasts. As much as I would like to attach certainty to one feast/festival over another, we really cannot. Like the Hebrew children who each year look to the sky for the Bridegroom of Creation, we also look, watch, and pray for the Bridegroom, believing he is on his way. Will he return? Yes! When? The signs show sooner than later. Even so come, Lord Jesus, come! Until then, learn to fill your days with the sacred.

Your Sacred Day

Before any feast came into existence, we had the sacred. We call it the seventh day, the day of rest. What do you do on your day of rest? Do you honor the Sabbath or Sunday?

The historic day is a Saturday. If you have no bend or flexibility in your relationship with God, you may be critical of those who choose Sunday as their holy day. Jesus handled the issue when he declared man was not made for the Sabbath, but the Sabbath was made for man.[13] The main point is, are you taking time each week to experience quality time with God? To be moved by the holy and renewed by the community of worshippers who honor the sacred one? Gathering together for this purpose was sanctioned by the writer of Hebrews, who challenged us not to forsake this activity. A command is directing more considerable importance to the church gathering as we see the day approaching.[14] Scripture calls us to focus and fine-tune our understanding around a one day a week gathering as intentional maintenance and a single-mindedness for worship and "The Day" of his return.

---

[13] Mark 2:27 NIV

[14] Hebrews 10:25 NIV

CHAPTER 6

Healing a Broken Culture

Woe to those who call evil good and good evil, who put darkness for light and light for darkness, who put bitter for sweet and sweet for bitter.[1]

Jeff Kinley in his book, *Wake the Bride*, addresses the broken culture and how groupthink processes today's culture. The flow of thought these days permeates postmodern Christian reasoning. It goes something like this, "You can't have 100 percent assurance of doctrine X, and it doesn't matter anyway if it's not essential to the faith." Assertions about absolute truth and, particularly, anything related to prophesy is deemed invalid since no one knows the future, right? Plus, the spirit of the age dictates that we display immediate skepticism against any form of spiritual dogma. Being confident regarding God's truth is often considered arrogant, narrow-minded, old school, unenlightened, and even mean-spirited. And this attitude exists not only in the secular world but within the Christian community as well.[2]

---

[1] Isaiah 5:20 NIV

[2] Jeff Kinley, *Wake the Bride*, 58.

Everyone is doing what's right in their own eyes; this leaves us with damaged people, broken systems, and a perverse culture. It's a world filled with others acting out against God's master plan. Don't let the culture keep you from finishing strong. Violators and perpetrators against children, women, and the innocent do distort our worldview. The Word of God was written to address every evil, heresy, false doctrine, and lie the world produces. A society looking for answers won't find them outside of God's Word. Isaiah prophesied about an upside/down world perspective. This prophecy is happening right before our very eyes. Here is my assessment of the possible fulfillment of these three prophecies.

1. **Calling good evil and evil good:** Biblical marriage is challenged, and same-sex marriage is accepted. Could this be the fulfillment of this prophecy?

2. **Darkness exchanged for light and light for darkness:** A cultural morality code is accepted as enlightenment, while biblical truth as darkness. Could this be prophecy fulfillment?

3. **Bitter for sweet and sweet for bitter:** The loss of innocence due to child trafficking, while more children are confused about their gender. Could this be the fulfillment of prophecy?

Isaiah's prophecy points to a society where confusion is the norm—where they are battling for the right to determine who declares what is truth. The same thinking applies to what is good or evil. In a fast-changing culture, the standards have become very fluid. Society has three options when it comes to laws.

Natural Law: A self-evident law with a belief system in an all-powerful law set in nature and given by a Creator. Gravity is an example—what goes up must come down. The pairing of animals is another example, as we need males and females to keep the species from extinction. Christians believe the Bible is based on this type of law, which was given to humanity. Our forefathers said our rights were self-evident, and they wrote the constitution based on that belief.

Totalitarian Law: A dictatorship functions and operates with the people at the top telling the masses what they can and cannot do. Marxism, Communism, and Islamic countries all live under this type of law.

Self-Governing Law: Don't confuse the name of this law with democracy. The book of Judges exposes the fallout when this kind of law governs the land and what it does to everyday people. Its premise is when everyone does what is right in their own eyes, people suffer.

Unless we are governed by an all-knowing, all-powerful, and immutable being who loves his creation, the society will continue to crumble. God gave us the Bible as a guidebook or manual for an abundant life and as a law that enables society to know its boundaries. The clarity of the Scriptures is unparalleled. The world is a broken system and is at a loss to what is a healthy society. Ambiguity seems to be a desirable outcome because the root of uncertainty lies within the heart. The Word of God reveals the heart; its thoughts and attitude. This is why society has turned against the Scripture. Those who do not honor God must attack the Word to justify their actions. They argue against creation saying, "If you're born a certain way, how can you be held accountable?" If we are God's creation and born in his image, then we are accountable to him. Unless you distort his image, starting with his Word.

Infallible

Words like inerrant or infallible are messing with the human reasoning. We see examples all around us reminding us that we make mistakes. Information continually alerts us to change. Eggs are bad for you. Update, eggs are good for you. Warning, eggs can be the wrong choice for your diet. Breaking news, eggs can be a healthy choice for your diet. Are there guidelines for authentic truth and stability in a Google-driven world?

Until the recent persecution of the Word, Scripture accurately handled was the anchor of scriptural interpretation. Now people are considered ignorant or less informed than those who use reason as the central evaluator. Younger peers have even laughed at the idea that Scripture could be supreme. How can holiness survive without a Holy Word? When searching for answers, some experts consult other sources outside of God's Word, which are considered most desirable, and the Word of God is often removed from the equation.

An Unsolved Question

Why doesn't God do something about the hurt, tragedies, and human suffering in the world? With all his power and love, how can these wrongs remain? Is it unfair or a cop-out to say he measures life and justice on the eternal scale? "For our light and momentary troubles are achieving for us an eternal glory that far outweighs them all. So we fix our eyes not on what is seen, but on what is unseen, since what is seen is temporary, but what is unseen is eternal."[3]

Every good story has its hero and its villain. Time is often the villain while waiting for God to heal your dying husband or to bring a job. Time is usually the way we decide if God loves us. When we let time be a part of the equation of God's goodness, love, or power, time will win, and our view of God becomes very twisted. God's measuring stick for justice is not the here and now but is in the eternal.

The following is a leadership question from a John Maxwell conference. Has time worn you down or polished you up? It is an excellent question for those wrestling with the truth of the Scriptures. When it comes to discovering the mysteries of the Word of God, time will be one of the stronger challenges to your faith. A sick spiritual cultural will attack the source of their healing.

Cultural Pull

Culture is the pulse of what is considered correct or proper in society today. It has the right to change when it wants. Cultural

---

[3]   2 Corinthians 4:17 NIV

norms to succeed must be played out in our Bible institutes as well. Here is some evidence it is happening. I will list the latest accusations against the Word of God. They may not seem like a big deal to some, when in fact this undermining of the Bible is a source of brokenness in our culture. If we label the foundation of truth as faulty, have we condemned the world to live in a falsehood? The latest heresies:

Adam and Eve are not real but an allegory of humanity. A simple study of the genealogies of the Bible will affirm Adam and Eve as real people.

The Exodus of Israel from Egypt was not a mass exodus. This logic asserts that the Sinai desert shows no evidence of millions of people living in it during the period of Moses's life. However, there has been no excavation done in the Sinai because its shifting sands make this difficult if not impossible to do. Lack of excavation is not proof it didn't take place. One author on the subject said it took them forty years to find a Jeep that was stranded in the Sinai.[4] The many Biblical as well as historical references give us no reason to question the validity of the mass exodus. The only other option is to discredit Moses and in doing so erase our source of wisdom from Heaven. The last two heresies we address, attempt to build such a case.

---

4 Richard Friedman, interview, "The Exodus Is Not Fiction," *Judaism Magazine*, 2013.

Moses was not the author of Deuteronomy.

Since Moses is credited with writing the first five books of the Bible, there is an agenda to discredit him. Current reasoning and recent Church history play a superior role in interpreting the Bible. Scripture is not even sought after as a support role. A couple of large church Pastors have recently been teaching we don't have to have the Bible to be a Christian. When new scholars use reasoning alone to assert that Moses isn't the author of Deuteronomy, we must ask what evidence the Scripture gives to refute such a claim.

In Joshua 8:31 (NIV), we find the command to build an altar with whole stones "as it is written in the book of the law of Moses." This command is found only in Deuteronomy 27:6.

Nehemiah 13:1 (NIV) tells us "read from the Book of Moses" that "no Ammonite or Moabite should ever enter the assembly of God." That command appears in Deuteronomy 23:3, and, thus, Deuteronomy is identified as the "book of Moses."

The disciples asked Jesus, "Why then did Moses command us to give a certificate of dismissal and to divorce her?" (Matthew 19:7, referring to Deuteronomy 24:1). Jesus responded, "Moses permitted you to divorce your wives because of your hard hearts, but from the beginning, it was not this way" (Matthew 19:8). This law appears exclusively in the book of Deuteronomy.

In Mark 12:19, we read of the Sadducees' discussion *with Jesus regarding the resurrection. They began,*

"Teacher, Moses wrote for us: 'If a man's brother dies and leaves a wife but no children, that man must marry the widow and father children for his brother," quoting Deuteronomy 25:5. The law is about the kinsman redeemer.

In John 5:46, Jesus said, *"If you believed Moses, you would believe me because he wrote about me." This refers to Deuteronomy 18:18, where Moses prophesies about the lamb of God.*

In Acts 3:22-23, Peter is quoted as *saying, "Moses said, 'The Lord your God will raise up for you a prophet like me from among your brothers. You must obey him in everything he tells you. Every person who does not obey that prophet will be destroyed and thus removed from the people." Peter was quoting Deuteronomy 18:15,19.*

In 1 Corinthians 9:9, Paul writes, *"For it is written in the law of Moses, 'Do not muzzle an ox while it is treading out the grain," quoting from Deuteronomy 25:4.*[5]

The Scriptures are the determining factor, and the answer is yes, Moses is the author of Deuteronomy. Could he have used a scribe to do the writing? This is a possibility and even likely. Jesus affirming Moses along with the apostles and several Old Testament figures settles the issue. It also goes to the

---

[5] Theosophical Ruminator, "Did Moses Write Deuteronomy?", under Bible Theology, (April 8, 2011).

establishment of tradition. Tradition is one leg of the stool that helps support Scripture. It also creates reasoning by validation of so many sources, and, therefore, the subject should be closed. Several scholars ignore these facts, for they no longer let Scripture determine the logic of their reasoning. Their argument is Moses dies in Deuteronomy 32 and there are two chapters after his death. The rumors of authenticity are mysteries we love to chase. With the due diligence displayed throughout the Scripture, the hunt should have ended. The simple answer is Moses, like many authors, used scribes to do their writings. Yet the message is getting louder from a liberal clergy; they want to prove the Bible is fallible. But rest assured, the Word of God anticipates all twists and curves.

A Holy Culture

The church of the Nazarene is where I gave my heart to Jesus. I became a part of a holiness movement. Holiness is not a common word. It is not used in social settings and rarely used in religious ones. The word holiness was set apart as one of the sacred words of the Bible. Holiness is God's vehicle for transformation in our lives. God is Holy and the only source of holiness.

Philosophies of God's limited power are taught today not as a theory, but as answers to our world's problems. This momentous error creates the removal of God as the answer to our culture. The holiness puzzle will not be solved outside of the attributes of God's omniscient, omnipresent, omnipotent powers. Holiness was never meant to travel solo. Holiness needs God's full abilities and attributes to be viable. I have found his all-knowing nature a vital piece of my life's puzzle; along with his Holy Word, they work as a guard against an unbiblical worldview. His omniscient power is one of the rejuvenating ingredients in holiness, for nothing sets God apart as God more than his ability to know the end from the beginning.

Why doesn't every Christian receive teachings about holiness as part of God's omniscient power? Our culture needs the church to step up and teach the truth, for the truth is the only thing capable of healing a broken culture.

Only the Creator Can Heal the Creation

Where do we get concepts of justice, good, evil, and morality? Somebody somewhere had to create the ideas of boundaries within society. They're a part of every civilization throughout history. If the source of good, evil, justice, and morality came from humans, can't humans change them as cultures change? Christians believe they are from God, grounding them in qualities of his consistency. Absolutes are essential promises to the believer, because our God doesn't change like shifting shadows.[6] God spoke through the Holy Spirit to obedient men and women who wrote the Bible, our moral code. Some want to immediately jump to Leviticus when we mention moral code.

The Levitical Law did its job well, pointing out the sinfulness of humanity and condemning us for it. But as powerful as it was, it was powerless in another way.[7]

---

6   James 1:11 NIV

7   Romans 8:3-4 NIV

The Bible is the only self-correcting book. The author of Hebrews gives us the amendments needed for the Levitical law— the adjustment made by God through Jesus, so society would not think strict adhering to the law was the answer to its needs. The book of Hebrews tells us that the old law was set aside "because it was weak and useless (for the law made nothing perfect)." The law had no way of changing our sinful nature. We needed something better to accomplish that.[8] We needed a savior, one who could redeem us from the sin and open our eyes to our need for wisdom and the purpose of the law.

Where do you get information? Authors, professors, pastors, television, or our iPhones are some sources. Where do those sources get their knowledge? The answer is academia. It's the learning of facts, details, formulas, and equations of a given subject. Information combined with experience creates a new level of understanding. I call it the revelation knowledge. It's when the light goes on in a mind, heart, and soul and the pieces come together, creating inner peace. The goal and the result is wisdom from Heaven. There are several kinds of wisdom; which are you striving to obtain?

Wisdom from Heaven

"Who is wise and understanding among you? Let them show it by their good life, by deeds done in the humility that comes from wisdom. But if you harbor bitter envy and selfish ambition in your hearts, do not boast about it or deny the truth. Such "wisdom" does not come down from heaven but

---

8   Hebrews 7:18-19 & https://www.gotquestions.org/Levitical-Law.html.

is earthly, unspiritual, demonic. For where you have envy and selfish ambition, there you find disorder and every evil practice. But the wisdom that comes from heaven is first of all pure; then peace-loving, considerate, submissive, full of mercy and good fruit, impartial and sincere. Peacemakers who sow in peace reap a harvest of righteousness."[9]

The ultimate healing of a broken culture is wisdom. The problem arises because there are many sources of wisdom. One source is earthly; it's not necessarily bad; it is just limited because it is temporal wisdom. Another reference is unspiritual. It also can seem innocent, but it lacks any input from God. The third kind James describes as demonic. This type of wisdom is rooted in twisting or perverting God's Word and will. James then tells us about a heavenly wisdom; the source is straight from God. It is pure, without a hidden agenda. Its goal is accomplishing a peace-loving outcome. It's considerate and submissive to others. It's full of mercy, and this wisdom would do wonders for our court system. The wisdom described by James has an outcome of righteousness. A right standing with God. There we have it. The solution to a broken culture is the Word of God, the will of God, and the wisdom of God guiding our lives.

---

[9] James 3:13-18 NIV

CHAPTER 7

⊛ 0 ⊛

The Bible within the Bible

*I wish that all the LORD's people were prophets and
that the LORD would put his Spirit on them!*[1]

When something is found within something, the term
is called inception. We know this as the dream
within the dream or the vision within a vision.
Isaiah is called the Bible within the Bible or our puzzle within the
puzzle. Isaiah contains sixty-six chapters. Thirty-nine chapters
have an Old Testament judgment and flare, while twenty-
seven chapters have insight into New Testament subjects such
as the suffering savior, grace, mercy, heaven, the tribulation,
and the new millennium. There are more in-depth descriptions
of Jesus in Isaiah than those found in the Gospels concerning
his character, suffering, and ruling of our world. The number
of chapters in Isaiah and their break, plus their themes, parallel
the Bible. Some scholars pay too much attention to Isaiah's
historical origins and not enough to its message. If you focus on

---

[1] Numbers 11:29 NIV

Isaiah as a historian, you will never catch the value and emphasis of his writings. There has never been a purer prophetic book through the Holy Spirit. Isaiah's prophecies pinpoint the future in many time periods, events, and people. It is amazing. When the Scriptures teach about God as the all-knowing, omniscient being of heaven, we find those facts revealed throughout the Bible but bookended by two essential books—one is Isaiah and the other is Revelation. This tandem of an Old Testament and New Testament book happens in another attribute of God. When looking at him as the all-powerful, omnipotent being of the universe with examples throughout the Scriptures, yet, this time Exodus and Acts act again as bookends to this characteristic.

If there were one book to study, it would be Isaiah. He uses pejorative language in describing Israel, their sins, and rebellion toward God. The extensive vocabulary is more significant than any other writer or book in all the Scriptures. The spot-on detail of civilization coming on the horizon as a future power makes this an excellent prophetic puzzle—a pure and holy servant of God that will die at the hand of one of the Kings of Israel. Historians say he was sawed in two. But oh, how he lived, and the messages within his book gives us the purest records of fulfilled prophecies. Isaiah is also one of the most futuristic voices for the 21st century. Isaiah details God's role for the future of his children's lives. He provides a prophetic breakdown of every significant event from Isaiah's time to the creation of a new heaven and a new earth. We will examine several of them, which will reveal an all-knowing God who uses the vehicle called prophecy.

The Father Voice

God doesn't want our sacrifices or our rituals. He desires for us to know him and his truth and follow his ways. In Isaiah, you will often hear the Father's voice talking to the children of Israel. You can feel his brokenness over their sins and their rejection of him. "Hear me, your heavens! Listen, earth! For the LORD has spoken: 'I reared children and brought them up, but they have rebelled against me. The ox knows its master, the donkey its owner's manger, but Israel does not know, my people do not understand.'[2] **Before Jesus introduced us to the Lord's Prayer,** Isaiah gives us a glimpse into the Father's heart. You can feel the pain and disappointment God is expressing about his chosen people. Animals know who takes care of them, loves them, and protects them. Israel either doesn't understand or is not willing to recognize who provides for them. Three hundred years earlier, God told them how special they are and that they are not like other nations. Other nations should be jealous of Israel, for they have God as their provider. Sadly, they cried out to give us a king like other nations. We want someone we can see and someone we can go to in our time of need. God's desire was for Israel to be a unique people who would set the standard for the world, they rejected the standard and their God at the same time. It was a personal dismissal of God the Father. They wanted what everyone else had; they wanted to be like everyone else. Isaiah divulges God anguish and disgust at their choices. But just like God while they are sinning, he's prophesying about the cure for Israel and their sin. 'Come now, let us settle the matter,' says the

---

[2] Isaiah 1:2-3 NIV

LORD. 'Though your sins are like scarlet, they shall be as white as snow; though they are red as crimson, they shall be like wool.'[3]

The power of those words should be quoted somewhere every week to let sinners know of the cleansing power of God. While Israel was looking to other nations to help them with their Assyrian problem, God was offering himself to them.

The Teacher's Voice

The best lessons taught are the ones you learn from your parents. My dad didn't raise me, but he did remind me of God's incredible grace on his deathbed. My last communication with him was as he was dying of lung cancer. He said the big "C" was taking him out. I told him I hate cancer. Dad smiled and said, "The big "C" is Christ; he's the one taking me out." The lesson I learned that day is parents who understand their role will always point their children to God, no matter what else is going on. It was a moment I will always treasure. My dad's last sentence to his family was, "Hey, everyone. Let's sing Amazing Grace." As his sisters and cousin started singing, my dad took his first breath in eternity, and I knew now God would be my father and teacher.

"Many peoples will come and say, 'Come, let us go up to the mountain of the LORD, to the temple of the God of Jacob. **He will teach us his ways**, so that we may walk in his paths.' The law will go out from Zion, the word of the LORD from Jerusalem."[4]

---

3   Isaiah 1:18 NIV

4   Isaiah 2:3 NIV

God promised to teach us his ways, so we could learn to walk in his paths. Learning the kingdom of God from God is a big challenge. God will use many tools to teach us his ways. The Scripture is a great tool, but so are the disappointments, open doors, and closed doors. God has the whole world at his disposal to teach us his ways. He has a blueprint of learning designed for each of us.

Isaiah Prophecies about Different Time Periods

Sometimes what may seem like a historical portion of Isaiah's writings is, in fact, pure prophecy. The events did happen, but many of them long after Isaiah's death. Some are about to come to pass in our future. These passages are prolific in resources to help us remember the God who is faithful, for he knows the end from the beginning.

1. **The Assyrian siege** (Isaiah Chapters 6-7 & 36-40) The Assyrians were famous for defeating their enemies through sieges. It is a cruel technique. You surround a city and cut off their water and food supply and literally starve them out. These chapters reveal God's faithfulness to Jerusalem. Israel, divided into the northern kingdom, had already come under the Assyrians. The reports of people eating their children during a siege reached Jerusalem, and the Assyrians are now surrounding their city. Isaiah the prophet records how King Hezekiah humbles himself and calls on the Lord. God hears the king's cry, and, as the prophecy foretold, Jerusalem's protection. The timeline of these events

is fascinating! Isaiah starts prophesying in 739 B.C., and the siege doesn't take place until 701 B.C.

2. **The Babylonian Captivity** (Isaiah 39:4-6) Strangers who are not even a world power come to Jerusalem, and King Hezekiah shows them all the gold and his blessings. The prophecy is about a nation called Babylon who will take them into captivity. This does not happen until 586 B.C., and Isaiah died more than a hundred years before this prophecy was fulfilled.

In his book called *The Mystery of the Shemitah*, Jonathan Cahn describes the 70 years of Israel in captivity, revealing why the period lasted 70 years and not one day longer. Israel had not honored God or his word during ten Shemitah, meaning they did not sell and trade according to biblical instructions. Therefore, they owed God ten Shemaiah's, and God brought judgment on the nation until the debt was settled.[5]

3. **Medes/Persians** Isaiah 45 is a prophecy about King Cyrus 150 years before he is born. When Cyrus takes Babylon captive, another prophet named Daniel is waiting for him. Daniel hands King Cyrus Isaiah's scroll, describing the king and calling him by name. The prophecy within that scroll was Israel would be free to go home and restore Jerusalem and rebuild the temple. How could one prophet have such accuracy

---

[5] Jonathan Cahn, *Mystery of the Shemitah*, 48.

and another prophet, Daniel, so trust God's Word to walk into the presence of a new conquering king and hand him the Scriptures? These events build the evidence we need today and verify why we can trust God and his Word. Babylon took the Israelites captive in 606 B.C. and the command to rebuild the temple from King Cyrus came in 536 B.C. Seventy years paid in full.

The Messianic Prophet

This is probably the best title for Isaiah. When reading chapters 50-66 of Isaiah, we see the all-knowing God once again. The details, especially in chapter 53, are some of the most profound prophetic Scriptures in the whole Bible. "Surely, he took up our pain and bore our suffering, yet we considered him punished by God, stricken by him, and afflicted. But he was pierced for our transgressions, and he was crushed for our iniquities; the punishment that brought us peace was on him, and by his wounds, we are healed. We all, like sheep, have gone astray, each of us has turned to our own way; and the LORD has laid on him the iniquity of us all. He was oppressed and afflicted, yet he did not open his mouth; he was led like a lamb to the slaughter, and as a sheep before its shearers is silent, so he did not open his mouth."[6] Isaiah is so convincingly pointing to Jesus it is said many Rabbi's will not read it. The description could be only the Messiah. Here is a brief list of Isaiah's acknowledgment of Jesus and his various titles.

---

[6]   Isaiah 53:4-7 NIV

1. **Sovereign Lord** – eighteen times
2. **Lord of Host or Lord Almighty** – sixty-two times
3. **Redeemer** – Thirteen times

Isaiah was not limited in his prophecies about events such as the dynasties we can verify. He records prophecies about the rapture, the tribulation, and the second coming and millennium life on earth. He also was the first to declare there will be a new heaven and a new earth over 800 years before John the apostle did so in Revelation 21:1

The Rapture

"But your dead will live, LORD; their bodies will rise—let those who dwell in the dust wake up and shout for joy—your dew is like the dew of the morning; the earth will give birth to her dead. Go, my people, enter your rooms and shut the doors behind you; hide yourselves for a little while until his wrath has passed. See, the LORD is coming out of his dwelling to punish the people of the earth for their sins. The earth will disclose the blood shed on it; the earth will conceal its slain no longer."[7]

We see three essential elements of the rapture. There is the rising of the dead, and his bride being hidden in her room until his wrath is done. The reason for the God's wrath coming on the earth is stated as sin. This Old Testament glimpse parallels Jesus teachings in the Gospels of Matthew and Luke.

---

[7] Isaiah 26:19-20 NIV

The Tribulation

'Make up your mind,' Moab says. 'Render a decision. Make your shadow like night—at high noon. Hide the fugitives, do not betray the refugees. Let the Moabite fugitives stay with you; be their shelter from the destroyer.' "The oppressor will come to an end, and destruction will cease; the aggressor will vanish from the land. In love, a throne will be established; in faithfulness, a man will sit on it—one from the house of David—one who in judging seeks justice and speeds the cause of righteousness."[8]

In Matthew, Jesus tells the Jews, "When you see the abomination that causes desolation in the temple,[9] run to the hills." This prophecy of the hills of Moab is where the Jews will hide from the anti-Christ while they wait for the Lord's return.

The Second Coming

"For to us a child is born, to us a son is given, and the government will be on his shoulders. And he will be called Wonderful Counselor, Mighty God, Everlasting Father, Prince of Peace. Of the greatness of his government and peace there will be no end. He will reign on David's throne and over his kingdom, establishing and upholding it with justice and righteousness from that time on and forever. The zeal of the LORD Almighty will accomplish this."[10]

The most famous quoted passage from Isaiah holds the truth of Jesus reigning from David's throne; it has not yet happened,

---

[8] Isaiah 16:3-5 NIV

[9] Matthew 24:15 NIV

[10] Isaiah 9:6-7 NIV

but we believe it is coming soon. It signals the period known as the second coming, where Jesus is physically here for one thousand years before the Great White Throne Judgment.

The Millennial Reign

"Never again will there be in it an infant who lives but a few days, or an old man who does not live out his years; the one who dies at a hundred will be thought a mere child; the one who fails to reach a hundred will be considered accursed. They will build houses and dwell in them; they will plant vineyards and eat their fruit. No longer will they build houses and others live in them, or plant and others eat. For as the days of a tree, so will be the days of my people; my chosen ones will long enjoy the work of their hands. They will not labor in vain, nor will they bear children doomed to misfortune; for they will be a people blessed by the LORD, they and their descendants with them. Before they call I will answer; while they are still speaking, I will hear. The wolf and the lamb will feed together, and the lion will eat straw like the ox, and dust will be the serpent's food. They will neither harm nor destroy on all my holy mountain,' says the LORD."[11]

Scholars point to this as the millennial time-period for several reasons. Children are being born, people are building their own homes, and there is still death. The order of natural things has reverted to the innocence of the garden of Eden. Therefore, the wolf and lamb will feed together, and the lion will eat straw.

---

[11] Isaiah 65:20-25 NIV

A New Heaven and a New Earth

Isaiah 65:17-19 – *"See, I will create new heavens and a new earth. The former things will not be remembered, nor will they come to mind. But be glad and rejoice forever in what I will create, for I will create Jerusalem to be a delight and its people a joy. I will rejoice over Jerusalem and take delight in my people; the sound of weeping and crying will be heard in it no more."* [12]

Anyone who has read Revelation has seen these words and promises. To think they came eight hundred years earlier reveals the divine integrated message the Holy Spirit uses to communicate truth. The book of Isaiah is a blueprint of God's plan, and it accompanies the books of Daniel and Revelation as futuristic, prophetic, apocalyptic writings. May the voice of the prophet be heard in all our churches.

---

[12] Isaiah 65:17-19

CHAPTER 8

A Prophetic Word

Psalm 37:30 (ESV)
*"The mouth of the righteous utters wisdom, and his
tongue speaks justice."*

Water is a gift from God. The piping or the conduit
is expensive, but it enables people not to haul
water any longer. God chooses to work through
people as conduits for his will. It is a mystery for sure, but we
are his vessels in many areas of service and ministry. Just as
you know you can be gouged by water companies, and there
are unscrupulous people who want to control others with the
mysteries of the kingdom. God designed a gift system to unify
and build up the believing community. Miracles, prophetic
words, and words of knowledge all are designed for this purpose.
We will look at the blessings and the challenges they bring and
why an all-knowing God would share such gifts with flawed
people?

What constitutes a prophetic word, a prophetic blessing, or
even prophetic language?

"A prophetic voice starts with a prophetic ear." ~ **Mark Batterson**

In the book *Whisper* by Batterson, he tells of seven different ways God communicates to people. The first and most often means of God speaking is through Scripture.[1] How can we be confident when someone speaks into our lives? When the mouths of the righteous speak wisdom where did they find their source? We who are Pastors, teachers and Bible study leaders must be confident in knowing God's voice. Often on a Sunday morning, I remind those attending how different the gathering of the people of God is than any other assembly. The church is a holy gathering, and in here we have holy prayers. In here we have a holy vocabulary. In here, we have sacraments and blessings that the world knows little about. It either doesn't understand them or may not have ever heard of them in a spiritual context. God speaks through his Word, his creation, through visions and dreams, open or closed doors of opportunities, and others. Recognizing the voice of God comes through an intimate relationship with him. Spiritual words and phrases guide us to supernatural living. Tom Cain is not an ordinary eighty-five who loves God's Word. He wrote a paper on spiritual terms every Christian should know. He graciously breaks down some of the holy words of our faith and their relationship to each other. Tom displays the traits of a true disciple. We must continue to grow and learn and challenge ourselves. In doing so, we set an example for others to follow. Tom actively shares his faith as a teacher and recovery group leader. When asked why he

---

[1] Mark Batterson, *Whisper,* 29.

still does so much, his simple reply is, "I love God and his Word. Why wouldn't I do what I can still do?" Why indeed! Certain words in the Scripture make up our holy language. Tom, shares his insight into this language.

"Theology for Dummies"

Salvation is God's plan to bring us back into fellowship with him. He made this possible by sending his Only Son, Jesus, to die on the cross as a sacrifice for our sins. Jesus's own blood is the price he paid to save us from a sinful life. God then miraculously raised him from the dead.

Justification is the first step in the salvation process. It is God's reply to us turning our back on a sinful lifestyle and accepting his Resurrected Son as our Lord and Savior. When we do that:

1. He wraps the Righteousness of Jesus (see Righteousness, below) around us;
2. He pardons all our past sins;
3. He adopts us into his spiritual family; and,
4. He sends The Holy Spirit to live within us, and
5. He offers us the ability to overcome the sinful nature we were born with.

Righteousness is doing what God tells us to do in his instruction book, The Holy Bible.

Sanctification, next in the Salvation process is God's reward for us when we give him control of our lives and allow his Spirit to completely fill us. When we do that, the indwelling Holy Spirit makes it possible for our efforts to overcome our sinful nature to become a reality; and the Spirit guides us so that our thinking and actions become progressively more and more like those of Jesus. This results in the development of Holiness of our own; and, the enjoyment of a sense of security and peace that passes all human understanding.

Holiness is loving what God loves and hating what God hates and living like we really mean it.

Glorification, the final step in the Salvation process, takes place when God calls his adopted children home to be with him. [2]

T. L. Cain 8/10/2016

Developing what I call holy conversation with God need not be in the mystical category. Holy conversation in my Catholic upbringing is held in the confessional box, while others talk directly to God. These types of communications are a regular part of growing in the knowledge of Jesus and his Word. We never should rush into his presence and give a few wish list items and tack on an amen. Learn to seek his wisdom, his heart, and his knowledge of life's issues. Let Scripture be your primary source

---

[2] Tom Cain, "Theology for Dummies," (August 10, 2016).

of hearing God's voice. He will speak through other modes, but they will never violate the Scriptures. Like my friend Tom, keep learning and growing.

Give Me an Ear

We have three exchange students living with us. They have many challenges, and it's more than learning a new language. Listening especially to English with all the idioms is a feat in itself. Our Chinese girls have a difficult time with specific expressions or sayings that can be taken literal and figurative. To distinguish between the two, you must listen to the context of the word, and this takes discernment and education. These two ingredients are essential for others not to slip into a prideful position thinking they are all-knowing in their ability to speak into a person's life.

The terminology is called **"a prophetic word."** It means to speak wisdom or insight into another person's life. Hearing from God on behalf of another person should come with a warning label. If what's shared is not based on Scripture, it could be a form of manipulation. I will illustrate this point through two personal experiences. First, the positive one—I met a sweet saint named Mary Duran, a four-foot-ten, powerful woman of God. When I was interviewing at her church, she came up to me and said, "God, told me to give you Romans 12:2 and you will know this is the church. You are to come here and lead it." Mary could not have known the Scripture she just gave me was my life verse. God gave it to me when I entered the ministry. "Do not conform to the pattern of this world, but be transformed by the renewing of your mind. Then you will be able to test and approve what God's will is—his good, pleasing and perfect will."

While pastoring, I also encountered the prophetic word in a confrontational moment. We were about to ordain a man called to preach who, in his early years, had a moral failure. He had fully repented and was being used mightily by God. The morning we were going to honor this man with the license a board member's spouse announced, "I have a word from God but didn't know what to do about it." She said God told her to tell me, and that I would know what to do with it. The phrase that kept coming to her mind was, "Now is not the time." This is often a technique to control the desired outcome by using God as the author of the information. Her heart could not justify a man with a failure being used by God.

I told her I knew exactly what God was trying to communicate. She smiled saying, "I thought you would." Her smile faded when I said, "God is affirming what we are doing this morning and that 'now is not the time' to question this man's anointing." This event happened over ten years ago. We ordained the man of God, and he's been traveling all over the world with a passion from God and for God. Of course, the woman who was trying to manipulate left the church. A prophetic word is never a tool for our own purpose. But know this first of all, that no prophecy of Scripture is a matter of one's own interpretation, for no prophecy was ever made by an act of human will, but men moved by the Holy Spirit spoke from God.[3]

---

[3] 2 Peter 1:20-21 NIV

Unsafe People

Caution, some dangerous people pretend to speak on behalf of God. A person, whether a man or woman, who has an agenda with a prophetic voice is unsafe. They use a prophetic word only to seek personal gain through such abilities. I say this as a warning to my Catholic friends who may not understand this section because of the lack of teaching about it in the church. Therefore, never trust a prophecy that comes with a date on it or an obligation to give money. Too many times, charlatans have used a prophetic word as an act of God to control others, with the sole purpose of financial gain through fear.

True prophets of God are unique people, but they shouldn't be selfishly motivated or desire to take advantage of others. The penalty for a mistake or getting a prophecy wrong was a death sentence in the Old Testament. If the job description for a prophet was posted on a church website and one of the qualifications were 100 percent accuracy. Not only that, but there was also a warning that if your proficiency fell short of the 100 percent, it would mean not only the end of their position, but the termination of the prophet's life. How many people would answer that call? It is with great humility and awe for the Word of God that someone answers the call to be a prophet. No one would seek this office if they knew what the calling of the prophet is all about. Does God give insight into people's lives as a prophetic word or what is also known as a word of knowledge? The answer is yes! When God does do this, he is trusting us as his holy messengers to intervene in people's lives. We should only see ourselves as a servant, and not a superior. If God uses you in this manner, He's the one communicating, you are just the conduit.

Supernatural Communications

God's supernatural ability is to know everything, and, therefore, nothing takes him by surprise. God speaks to us and through us more often than we know. His mode of doing this is usually consistently through dreams, but he has been known to talk through a donkey[4] to the prophet Balaam or a burning bush as he did to Moses in the desert.[5]

I will pour out my Spirit on all people. Your sons and daughters will prophesy, your old men will dream dreams, your young men will see visions."[6] Joel, the prophet, describes a future where prophecy is a regular part of life. Our sons and daughters will be able to understand prophecy and, yes, to even speak a prophetic word. Their ability to hear from God will most often come through visions or dreams.

My encounters with prophetic visions are amazing and humbling. Like the promise from the book of Joel, it all started with a vision during a dream. A vision within a dream is what happened to Joseph. In Genesis, he was given a peek of his future as a seventeen-year-old. It was about his father, mother, and his brothers bowing down to him.[7] The problem with glimpses are the details you don't see. My dream was a lot more disturbing than Joseph's, and my response was, "Wow, what a horrible dream!" In the morning, the dream was still so vivid, and I prayed

---

4   Numbers 22:28 NIV

5   Exodus 3:4 NIV

6   Joel 2:28 NIV

7   Genesis 37:9-10 NIV

as God prompted me to for my friend whose life could be in danger. All day long, there was this overriding feeling, action needs to happen but, what? So when in doubt, pray for clear direction. I prayed, "Lord, protect my friend from the things you revealed to me in my dreams last night, and if you want me to contact him, give me that dream again tonight." Going to sleep that night there was peace in my heart; if God didn't speak to me about my friend, I would be off the hook.

Transforming the Mind

The mind has a conscious and a subconscious partnership. Dreams are a fantastic part of our spiritual life and the subconscious. Often my prayers before sleeping go like this. "Lord, you are God of my conscious mind and my subconscious mind. If there is anything you want to communicate to me during my sleep, let me know it's from you."

The dream came back, and the details still haunt me to this day. My friend was sitting in his basement in Philadelphia; it's a beautiful basement, one I've been in many times. He seemed to be very distraught, and there on his lap was a gun. A few minutes later he picked up the gun put in his mouth and shot himself. Immediately, I sat up in bed, raced to the phone, and called my friend. When he answered, he seemed surprised to hear my voice. My quick question was, "Are you ok?" He then started to ask me questions. "Why do you ask?" and "Why are you calling me so early in the morning?" I cut right to the chase and said, "God gave me a dream about you two nights in a row, so what's going on?" He was crying at this point saying, "Really, God put me in your dreams two nights in a row?" "Yes," I yelled, with my emotions fully engaged at this point. He said he had been crying out to God for the last two nights in his basement because he had just learned of his wife's affair with a guy from work. He said, "I so wanted to believe God was real and I was asking him to reveal himself to me. The devil was real. He was tormenting me greatly over the last two nights. It was horrible."

He then asked what happens in my dreams. I told him the truth, and his reply was, "I've been sitting here the last two nights asking God if he is real." I learned there was no gun, but the hurt was real. It was not the first time God used me or talked to me. It also wasn't going to be the last time.

Trust God, Not Your Emotions

God doesn't use prophecy to control people's choices, but to guide them to his purpose and plan. When your emotions are raw, it can be very hazardous to move in a prophetic realm. I will share how during the bleakest time in my adult life God used a prophetic word to guide me. We can never put God in a box.

God will work with any person as a vessel, and he will even talk through a donkey when a human being isn't available. Even when it is difficult to believe in yourself because of past failures, God is still willing to speak into and through your life. I speak from firsthand experience, as my Church saw me through divorce, singleness, and even falling in love again. This is the backdrop of God's encounter with another prophetic dream I had about my future. In the dream, I received details about a brunette who loved God and ministry. God was preparing me for a future step in my life. Yes, the brunette has now been my wife for over twelve years. The most remarkable part is God prophesied to her the year before I would meet her.

No supernatural knowledge validates divorce and the destruction it brings to the marriage and a family. It does, though, reveal an all-knowing God who gives hope even in the darkest settings. Mindy was dealing with the most painful trial of as her life as Tom her husband was dying of cancer. Mindy would have never believed such a thing could happen to her. She was praying for her husband and journaling about God's faithfulness. When God spoke to her heart and said, "If I had a broken pastor who had lost his wife and his church, could you come alongside and encourage him?" While sharing her experience with her dying husband, Tom said, he knew what God was up too. He told her God was preparing her for her next husband. She said, "But that's not my focus or even something I think about." Tom held her and they both cried. He said, "I have only two concerns when I am gone—that's you and Hannah. I believe one day you would make a perfect Pastor's wife." Then he smiled and reminded Mindy about how she enjoyed sitting in the front row of the church.

Mindy's life was one of a conservative church attender and she had never heard of things like prophecies. Her crisis enabled God to introduce her to his all-knowing power and love. Even during a time of profound loss, God shared a prophetic glimpse of hope—and what would one day be one of my greatest blessings.

Prophetic Blessing

Many blessings are wrapped up in tragedy. The template of a prophetic blessing came from God the Father when he spoke a prophetic blessing over Abraham.

The angel of the LORD called to Abraham from heaven a second time and said, 'I swear by myself, declares the LORD, that because you have done this and have not withheld your son, your only son, I will surely bless you and make your descendants as numerous as the stars in the sky and as the sand on the seashore. Your descendants will take possession of the cities of their enemies, and through your offspring all nations on earth will be blessed, because you have obeyed me."[8]

Isaac gives a blessing over Jacob and Esau, and if you research the Genesis account, you will see how every blessing for Israel came into being. When Jacob was old and ready to leave this world, he called in his twelve sons and spoke a prophetic blessing over each one. The Blessing of Jacob is a prophetic poem that appears in Genesis at 49:1-27 and mentions each of Jacob's twelve sons.

The void in so many of our children's lives is the blessing they need from their fathers. Fathers not trained in this biblical knowledge and the truth about blessing their children are missing out on a privilege and obligation to impact the next generation.

My oldest son is a newbie lead pastor. As he was moving into his office in the spring of 2017, I shipped several boxes of books to him. One set was a volume of 12 biblical, theological, ecclesiastical, encyclopedias written by Strong's and McClintock in 1890. They came from my professor, Milo Arnold, who became a spiritual leader to me. I can still see Professor Arnold standing in front of our class weeping over us, his future preachers

---

[8]   Genesis 22:15-18 NIV

to the world. The class was called. "The Making of a person who will become a Minster." He prayed in every session a blessing over us. Milo Arnold's life lives on because of his blessings over those students. We need mentors, coaches, and encouragers in our lives. In addition, we need the anchors of prophetic blessings in our lives. Five years after my graduation from college, my professor was diagnosed with Alzheimer's and was sent to a nursing home in Longview, Washington to be near his sister. She, Pearl Dixon, was the associate pastor of the church. I would be added to the staff of that church when they called me to be the youth pastor.

I started my preaching ministry in the nursing home, and each day I would see my professor slumped over in his wheelchair. He would have a few moments of clarity and then slip back into the faraway world of that cruel disease. One day while sitting with him, he looked at me. It was a day when I was questioning ministry and the personal cost it brings to one's life. Professor Arnold said, "You're one of my students." He said this on most visits, and the conversation rarely went much further. On this day God gave him a prophetic word for me. Milo said tenderly, "You are thinking about being in ministry?" I was shocked at his question and answered with a loud, "YES." He said, "Don't be in the ministry, for if you are in the ministry, you can get out. Become the ministry, and you will never get out." How did this man get a moment of clarity? The truth he shared sustained me through so many ups and downs in a highly visible profession called the clergy. It became the anchor in my life and calling. Indeed, it was a prophetic word for a young youth pastor who is eternally grateful.

The Power of Blessing

My hope is to one day leave a prophetic blessing over my sons, Shawn, Chris, and my step-daughter Hannah. To establish them with God's fulfillment and blessings adds a piece to their puzzle in this life. I want it to be more than just a reminder of God's goodness and greatness. I want it to be a word from God's heart, to my heart, to their hearts. I want this blessing to be a fulfillment of how God keeps his Word, and hopefully one day their children can experience a holy moment.

We need surrogate fathers to a whole generation—those who will sense the awe of God's calling in their lives and won't take this role lightly. When I was coming back to the church of the Nazarene, my spiritual father, Jack Eyestone, spoke into my life. He's played a role in dozens upon dozens of pastors, staff, evangelists, and even other district superintendents lives. He just recently retired from pastoring at age 82 and is still at his post of encouraging. Each week before moving back to the farm, he spoke words of affirmation and love to each pastor in the Inland Empire. His encouragement in my life caused me to come back to the church of the Nazarene. He has always been aware of my calling to be a pastor/prophet to the people. He said the church needs prophets today more than ever, and you need a platform. Anyone can be who they are supposed to be when it's easy. Jack reminded me prophets weren't often called to speak to people who are good at listening. We must encourage others to step out and lean heavily on faith in the supernatural God who speaks blessings. The prophetic word is part of the arsenal to combat the lie of our enemy, who wants to keep us from God's blessings.

CHAPTER 9

⮾

Keys to the Final Puzzle (Revelation)

The Revelation of Jesus Christ, which God gave unto him, to shew unto his servant's things which must shortly come to pass; and he sent and signified it by his angel unto his servant John:[1]

Some unique people can put a puzzle together upside down without seeing the picture. This rarity or skill is not possible with the biblical puzzle of the book of Revelation. Knowing the big picture is imperative to the book of Revelation. Keeping the focus as the portrayal or revelation about Jesus allows me to keep the theme as a point of reference.

Jesus is the subject of the final puzzle and the book of Revelation. We are told so in the first sentence. It's about his glory, message, wrath, and his return and reign on the earth. The acknowledgment of our Savior as the Alpha and the Omega. The Lord God, "Who is and who was and who is to come, the

---

[1] Revelation 1:1 NIV

Almighty." John, the writer of Revelation, is told twice to "write what you have seen." The mysteries of revelation are real. The subjects are in order of importance, Jesus, the church, Israel, the world, and eternity. The book contains seven intimate letters from Jesus to the seven churches of Asia Minor. Some scholars differ on this point, but I believe they were real churches. Prophetically, they represent every church that exists in every age. Chuck Missler and Bill Salus do a more exhaustive study in "The Seven Letters of Revelation."[2] Here is a summary of their work.

1. **The church of Ephesus** is the apostolic Church in every age. This represents people answering the call to follow Jesus. Reconciliation to God and each other is their primary goal.

2. **The church of Smyrna** is the persecuted church. Every generation has their list of martyrs of the faith.

3. **The church of Pergamum** is the church married to the world, and its principles.

4. **The church of Thyatira** is the works-based church. It is often identified as today's Catholic church. It is set up in the temple model. Salvation is through the sacraments and the need for an intercessor between God and humanity.

5. **The church of Sardis** is the church of reformation. Salvation is by faith, but it is a dead faith. They have a form of godliness but deny its power.

---

2 Chuck Missler and Bill Salus, "The Seven Letters of Revelation."

6. **The church of Philadelphia** is the missional church. They send missionaries to all parts of the world proclaiming the good news.

7. **The church of Laodicea** is the social gospel church. It is lukewarm because its emphasis is on social justice issues and not true salvation (the apostate Church).

He who has an ear, let him hear what the Spirit says to the churches.[3]

The letters to the churches in Asia minor are red-letter messages from Jesus. This means they are in a red print, showing this is Jesus's conversation to the churches. Tony Campolo, who coined the phrase Red-Letter Christians, wrote a challenge to the church in the 20th century.[4] He challenged the churches to a radical discipleship and obedience. Sadly, Tony was one of the leading pastors to endorse same-sex marriage. I personally wrote him and asked him to reconsider his position. His replied that he would pray over it. Two years have gone by and he still has not publicly changed his stance. Is this in part a representation of the great falling away Jesus spoke of in Matthew? Jesus engages us in truths and anchors each of them so that the culture we live in will not destroy us.

---

[3] Revelation 2:7 NIV

[4] Tony Campolo, Redleterchristians.org.

Ephesus

Jesus is the anchor of the church. He identifies himself as the one who holds the seven stars in his right hand and walks among the seven golden lampstands.[5] The fact that Jesus holds the seven stars in his right hand shows control and authority over the message and the messengers to the seven churches. The most recognizable message for the Christian church is love. It can be a dangerous statement unless we clarify it as agape love. In the name of love, people are living together in sin. They are taking marriage vows with partners of the same sex. Our first love is Jesus. The attack against love comes from a group called the Nicolaitans. They wanted to modernize and improve the Bible to be more acceptable to humanity. Jesus gives us a three-part solution to the sin within the church of Ephesus.

1. **Remember,** he has not moved away from us.
2. **Repent,** turn away from the falsehood and the things robbing you of devotion to him.
3. **Renew** your mind with the word and move out of love for Jesus to obedience.

Being Christlike and being biblical cannot be separated. Jesus is called the Word. This has deep-rooted implications. First, Jesus is asserting that when you read the Word of God, you're reading about him and his ways and his life. Second, just as there is no flaw or sin in Jesus, neither is there a flaw in his Word. A

---

5   Revelation 2:1 NIV

fundamental practice of believing the Bible only happens because of its authenticity. The Bible is never in question. We who are interpreting it are the ones whose validity should be questioned. Many have left their first love of Jesus and his Word. They fell for the cultural flaw of wanting to be relevant and, in doing so, lost their relevancy.

Smyrna/Pergamum

These two churches of Smyrna and Pergamum are a contrast to each other. Smyrna, as a church has many disparities of its own. It is a church without many resources, yet Jesus calls them rich. They are a people that will be thrown into prison, and, again, Jesus says don't worry about that because you are free. Jesus is proud of the Smyrna Church because their belief resulted in obedience. The importance of that truth cannot be overstated. The devil believes in God, but he is never obedient to him. The community within this church went beyond their knowledge or even logic to a total abandonment of trust in Jesus even to the point of death. Don't be confused. Your belief in God is vital, but it will always be secondary to your obedience to him. To the persecuted church (Smyrna), Jesus identifies himself as one who has the words of him who is the first and the last, who died and came to life again.[6] He identifies immediately with their fears of death and reminds them, you will come to life again. He gives this Church a great promise as they overcome the challenges of their day. They will not be

---

[6] Revelation 2:8 NIV

hurt by the second death.[7] Now, let's be honest—the reassurances of Jesus are needed. But he told them they would go to prison, and some would die. No one wants to accept those words as their main message from Jesus, yet it was his primary message to Smyrna. We like a gospel that spells out all our benefits. The good news to this portion of the body of Christ is I've got you for eternity.

Now we move quickly to the church of Pergamum as the contrast to Smyrna. It is a church that wanted to be accepted by the world so badly, and it compromised the gospel. Even worse, it added deception to the church. Jesus identifies himself to them as the one who has the sharp, double-edged sword.[8] We know the term refers to the Word of God from Hebrews. The word of God that is living and active.[9] Pergamum is drawn by the marvels of growing a worldly kingdom but not to the holiness of God. They loved it when society recognized the good of the church. They could not handle it when the Scriptures came into conflict with their cultural ways, so they compromised to be accepted by their peers and the intellects of their time. Pergamum's worst offense was it taught disregarding the Word of God as the authority. Corrupt teachers marked this church. Their teachings led people to believe you can be spiritual and not follow the Word of God. Your sexual choices were a part of your liberty. It sounds a lot like so many Christians circles who are accepting a homosexual lifestyle as a practice not under the judgment of God. Jesus warns

---

[7] Revelation 2:11 NIV

[8] Revelation 2:12 NIV

[9] Hebrews 12:4 NIV

that if this Church does not repent, he will come soon and fight against them with the sword of his mouth.[10] It may sound like the church of Pergamum is nothing but another religion, but within its community, there is a remnant of faithful followers of Jesus who will not renounce their faith. Jesus gives the latter a promise of hidden manna, which is a reference to the bread from heaven given to Israel during their time in the wilderness. Manna can also be considered the Word of God, which humanity needs to sustain life. The hidden aspect tells me this church's remnant will have unique insight and knowledge into the Word of God. If ever a people need such revelation, it would be a church swallowed up by the culture and intellects of its day.

Thyatira

The Thyatira church represents in the seven ages of the church the universal Church. Some call it the Catholic Church, which it could be, but for our purposes, we will keep it more general. Thyatira is the first Church in Revelation where Jesus, who has been describing himself with different attributes, declares his ultimate title, the Son of God.[11] Jesus addresses a grievous offense. The church has been listening to the spirit of Jezebel who leads them into sexual immorality.[12] If ever there was a prophetic message to the church, this is one we can clearly see. Many mainline movements have believed this deceptive spirit and are ordaining men and women that are openly

---

[10] Revelation 2:16 NIV

[11] Revelation 2:18 NIV

[12] Revelation 2:20 NIV

immoral according to God's Word. Jesus said he had given her time to repent, but the church was unwilling.[13] An open attack from Jesus himself is the result of a Church who enthusiastically embraces a sinful culture ideology. He adds a purpose behind his discipline of this church. "Then the church will know that I am he who searches hearts and minds, and I will repay each of you according to your deeds."[14] This is a warning to the rest of the church to not learn these ways of deceptions. This is the first time Jesus ever told his body a sin of Satan's deception has crept inside of you. Through the ages, we have seen many deceptions attack the church. The difference this time is a penalty of striking our children dead.[15] In an age where schools and culture are forcing deviant sexual manners as the norm, there is a prophetic warning from Jesus that this practice will mean death to our children. As always, the plea to the churches is do you have ears? Are you listening? The Spirit of the living God is giving warnings.

> To each church, Jesus uses the same phrase, "these are the words of him."

> He who is the authority and the central part of the church.

> He who is the first and last, who has the sharp double-edged sword.

---

[13] Revelation 2:21 NIV

[14] Revelation 2:23 NIV

[15] Revelation 2:23 NIV

He who the son of God, the fullness of God and the church.
He who holy and true, faithful and the ruler of creation

His descriptions provide a solution for every area of trouble that will come against the church. Jesus's answer to the church in every generation is to be the body of Christ. The remaining three churches receive a personal message from Jesus pertaining to their part in the community of believers.

Sardis

Delimar's remains were never found. They were thought to have been incinerated. For six years, Luz Cuevas had a niggling doubt about whether her ten-day-old daughter Delimar Vera had perished in a fire in their Philadelphia home late in 1997. Her doubt was confirmed when in 2004 at a birthday party, Cuevas noticed a six-year-old girl who resembled herself and her two children. Cuevas reportedly managed to take some strands of the girl's hair under the ruse of stuck bubblegum, and DNA proved she was, in fact, her daughter. She'd been kidnapped by a recent acquaintance, Carolyn Correa, who started the fire and raised Delimar as her own. Cuevas was reunited with Delimar in 2004.[16] These once thought dead and are alive true-life stories are heartrending, but Jesus's message to people who believe they are alive but dead brings eternal consequences.

You have a reputation of being alive but are dead.[17] Jesus is not known for his Dale Carnegie technique on how to win

---

[16] Jim Mitchell, "Out the Fire," (July 2016).

[17] Revelation 3:1 NIV

friends and influence people. He doesn't sugar coat his message to the church. God judges the church not on its reputation but on its deeds. Yes, this means to feed the poor, clothe the naked, and much more. Dead people spiritually can do those tasks and many others, including being a good neighbor, but the message embodies being a good ambassador. The call is to "Wake Up." How have we gone to sleep? The church asleep at the wheel in the last days is such a huge problem. I am taking all of Chapter eleven to address it. The confrontation goes beyond waking up. It's a threat of missing his second coming because they lost the very essence of who he is to this world.

Therefore, Jesus reminds the church he is the fullness of the Spirit. He knows their deeds and declares they are unfinished in the sight of God.[18] A false and very deceptive teaching has invaded the church, stating if you feed the hungry and clothe the naked, you've earned salvation. God sees our deeds and declares they aren't enough. There is something more to being a good neighbor, and it's a good witness while giving testimony of Jesus as your Savior. Social justice while important will never replace the gospel. To do both is Christianity at its finest.

What Jesus describes in Sardis is reminiscent of our late-night horror shows. He is portraying spiritual zombies, Christians who are walking and acting in the name of Jesus, but they are dead and have soiled clothes.[19] The clothing is a clue that what is done in the name of Jesus has no merit. Desiring this more, Jesus points to a remnant living in obedience to his will. There

---

[18] Revelation 3:2 NIV

[19] Revelation 3:4 NIV

has been in every age a church that has been a remnant living out God's plan for humanity. This could point to the prophetic side of Jesus message to the churches. The promise to the faithful is their name will never be blotted out, and Jesus will acknowledge them before his Father and the angels.[20] This is a reference to judgment day.

Philadelphia

Never has one segment of the church been elevated as the church of Philadelphia. The greater obedience you live in, the higher the revelation of the character of God—the words of him who is holy and true, who holds the key of David. What he opens no one can shut, and what he shuts no one can open.[21] Only Yahweh is holy and true. Jesus is again admitting he is God. Being Holy and True is more than tendencies learned; they are attributes of his being. He admires Philadelphia's ability to keep his Word. This could be the reason there is an open door for them no one can shut. The privilege of open doors of opportunity comes to those who keep his Word. Have you ever tried to open doors of opportunity and no matter how hard you worked, nothing would come to pass?

Missionary David Livingstone knows the reality of an open door and a closed door. It's fitting to bring a missionary into Revelation, and the church of Philadelphia is classified as the missional church in the world. Livingstone is famous for his years of service in Africa, but it was the shut door to China that allow

---

[20] Revelation 3:5 NIV

[21] Revelation 3:8 NIV

Robert Moffat to tell David tales of enchantment about the move of God in the deep bush of Africa. This was David's opening to create God's highway through over 1,500 miles from South Africa through the interior of Africa with the Gospel of Jesus. The open door was also to the heart of his boss's daughter, Mary Moffat, who became David Livingstone's wife.[22]

A significant promise to the church beyond rewards is the promise as it overcomes the obstacles and sins in this world. It's not a promise of something they would receive, but something they could escape. I will keep you from the hour of tribulation that is come on the whole world to test the inhabitants of the earth.[23] These Christians are being offered an exemption to the test. The only way to escape is not to be inhabiting the earth; sounds like a rapture to me. The message to Philadelphia ends with the sequential listing of events that follow their removal from the earth. He is coming soon, a judgment and new names and a new Jerusalem coming down out of heaven. Jesus enjoys sharing future events with his faithful followers; this is a pattern you can trace back to his message in the last week of his life.

Laodicea

In culinary terms, no one can agree on what dictates a lukewarm status. Some mark lukewarm at the body temperature or approximately 98.6°F. Others say it is room temperature. Room temperature, of course, varies, but most agree it is from 72°F to 74°F (sometimes up to 78°F). Still others say lukewarm is room

---

[22] Christian History, "David Livingstone," (1997).

[23] Revelation 3:10 NIV

temperature plus about 15 degrees. Lukewarm and tepid are considered synonyms.[24]

I like my ice cream cold, and I love my hot chocolate extra hot, so the marshmallows are melting. This makes me feel more like Jesus. It's probably the easiest way to associate myself with him. "To the last church in Revelation, these are the words of the Amen."[25] Amen has two English meanings. The first is "Let it be so." The second is what I believe this passage is declaring, "It is so." You can sense Jesus's tenderness in communicating with his body, the church. Yet there is this resolution of clarity in his stance about obedience.

It's tempting to not even address this issue within the church, with all the inclinations this subject can stir. Calling himself the ruler of God's creation sets in motion a final message to the church. Whose creation? The ruler of God's creation is not future tense. It is a demonstrative statement of a fact. The church in the 21st century is at room temperature on this subject. I see Jesus putting it right out there for them by saying I wish you were either cold on this or hot. Pretending this is not important to get right is not pleasing to God. He reserved the harshest and the most extensive list of rebukes for this church and the age it represents. He gives them an extensive counseling session on making changes. The offer to this church is a God willing to come in and renew fellowship. My prayer and hope is that this generation will accept that offer and a new day of serving and obedience will be birthed.

---

[24] Eric Troy, "What is the Temperature of Lukewarm," (January 13, 2015).

[25] Revelation 3:14 NIV

The Key

Whenever you hear the word key, are you like me, immediately wanting to know what it unlocks? Remember, curiosity is imperative to the spirit of a prophet. My friend Pete Stephens allowed me to borrow his master's level commentary on Revelation. I would like to address why we refer to this book as the "Apocalypse." Can associations with other parts of the Bible help us interpret the book of Revelation? Why would God give a special blessing to the readers of this book? If we view Revelation so different from other books in the Bible, could it be misinterpreted? Can commentaries be misleading when it comes to prophesy and the Bible? I am going to pick on one analysis and use it as an example when interpreting Revelation. This commentary is used at a seminary to educate our young clergy in understanding the book of Revelation. I could not address the entire commentary, but its premise gives you the feeling it is locked up tighter than a drum. Some of their comments leave you feeling the key may have never even been made to unlock the mysteries of this book. For this reason, I want to discuss the power we give books, commentary, and pastors/teachers over Scripture interpretation. This applies to all that I've written and researched. None of this should trump what Scripture itself reveals.

Smyth & Helwys Bible Commentary on Revelation
No New Testament writing other than Revelation belongs to the literary genre of apocalypse. (The only example in the Hebrew Bible is the book of Daniel.) Thus, when readers encounter the book of Revelation, they are dealing with a genre generally unfamiliar to them.

The word "apocalypse" comes from the opening word in the Greek text of Revelation, *apokalypis,* which means "revelation." Apocalyptic literature, then, is revelatory literature; it is literature that claims to reveal cosmic secrets to a human recipient. These secrets usually involve information about otherworldly regions (heaven, hell, the places of the dead, the outer regions of the earth), and/or events of the final days (the destruction of the world, the last judgment, rewards of the righteous, and punishment for the wicked). Typically, apocalypses contain an otherworldly figure (such as an angel) who serves as a mediator of the revelation given to the earthly recipient. [26]

I agree that the identification of prophecy is unfamiliar to most Bible readers. Their language of secrets involving information from otherworld regions is an accurate concept. I am not here to discredit any commentary but to help us see that often they influence us more than the Bible influences us itself. Let's examine some assumptions from the introduction. What reasoning are they using to isolate Revelation and its connection from all the other literature in the Bible except the book of Daniel? Their reasons are in bold, while Scripture and my reply or refutation is ordinary text.

1. **Cosmic secrets are given to a human recipient.** (This is true of the whole Book of Job and Genesis chapters 1-11. It is also in Isaiah chapters 1, 50-53, 60-66, and many numerous passages in Psalms. This is also found in Romans chapters 1, 2, 5, 6, 8 and Luke 1 with

---

[26] Smyth & Helwys Bible Commentary on Revelation, 35.

the Virgin Mary, and Zechariah) The author only mentioned the distinction between Revelation and Daniel.

2. **Information about otherworldly regions of heaven, hell, the places of the dead, the outer regions of the other.** (Again, Job, Psalms, Proverbs, Isaiah, Jeremiah, Ezekiel, and Zechariah. Jesus's teaching in the Gospels gives us a detailed description of hell. Paul describes a trip to heaven.)

3. **Events of the final days, the destruction of the world, judgment, and the punishment of the wicked.** (Noah's story in Genesis chapters 6-9, Isaiah chapters 1-39, Psalms 2, Romans chapter 2, Jude, I Peter, 2 Peter, 2 Thessalonians 2) Again, the author only mentions Daniel.

4. **Otherworldly figures such as angels who serve as a mediator of revelation given to an earthly recipient.**

   The Old Testament:
   Adam and Eve encounter the serpent.
   Hagar encounters an angel.
   Jacobs encounters an angel of the Lord.
   Job encounters God.
   Gideon encounters an angel.
   Moses encounters God.
   Joshua encounters the angel of the Lord.
   Elisha and his servants encounter thousands of angels.

The New Testament:
The virgin Mary encounters Gabriel, along with
her relative Zechariah visit with Gabriel.
Joseph encounters an angel.
The apostle Paul encounters Jesus after his
ascension.
Peter encounters an angel in prison and on a
rooftop.
An angel speaks to Phillip,
This is not an exhaustive list, but you can see
Revelation does connect with the rest of Bible.

Generalities about Revelation is wrongly separating it from the Bible and has consequences. Many young clergies are afraid to preach and teach from it. One seminary graduate who is a pastor exclaimed, "I will never preach from Revelation." Our world and people need the full counsel of God's Word.

A great rule of thumb when interpreting Scripture is to verify other writings and commentaries against the Word of God. If we isolate the Book of Revelation from the knowledge in the rest of the Bible, we will get bizarre or wrong interpretations of Revelation.

There are verses in Revelation that are in the categories of allegory and are symbolic. The symbols in the Bible are more common than most teachers want us to believe. As previously stated, Christians associate the word dove with the Holy Spirit; they associate snake, dragon, or serpent with the devil; and they associate Lamb of God with Jesus. Many godly pastors like David Jeremiah have written excellent books on

Revelation. The commentary didn't want to address the obvious. Revelation is a glimpse into future prophetic events. Leaving this description out causes them to view many passages as historical and without a future fulfillment. We must be careful not to handle prophetic Scripture as overly unique. At one time, all the prophecies concerning Jesus, the Jewish people, and our present world were the basis of futuristic prophecies in the Word.

Timing and Revelation

An example is when Ezekiel asked, "Can these dry bones live again?"[27] This question was asked hundreds of years before Jesus birth. Being blessed with the power of history on our side, we can see a nation dispersed for almost two millenniums come to back to life. When Israel became a nation in May 1948, we could reach back through the ages and bring Ezekiel to a modern-day understanding. Without the nation's birth, this could not have happened. During the six-day war in June 1967, Jerusalem was once again captured and became the capital city of Israel. Another stage is complete in the almost fully resurrected Israel. The missing piece is to rebuild their temple for the third time. Until that happens, we can only speculate on many of the future events. The timing issue is not critical. Many like to contemplate and armchair quarterback what the Holy Spirit is up to. These things can take you off the focus of the final piece, which is Jesus. He is incapable of lying. He has made promises to his bride. The day is always closer than the day before. The

---

[27] Ezekiel 37:3 NIV

secret is to watch Israel but keep your eyes on Jesus, the author and finisher of our faith.[28] When you do this, new revelation knowledge comes to you.

---

[28] Hebrews 12:2 NIV

Chapter 10

The Christmas Prophet

But as for you, Bethlehem Ephrathah, too little to be
among the clans of Judah, from you One will go forth
for Me to be ruler in Israel his goings forth are from
long ago, From the days of eternity.[1]

Daniel the prophet and many of his young Jewish friends couldn't imagine why they would never see home again. He was only seventeen when kidnapped by the Babylonians who took Israel into captivity. He was selected because he showed skills in the sciences, astrology, astronomy, and probably even soothsaying. The Hebrew definition for soothsaying was someone who tells the truth. How ironic that being a good student and bright kid made you a top choice for an enemy to take you to their country for the rest of your life? Daniel and friends no doubt suffered many seasons of homesickness in their new environment. He would never experience another holiday or holy day in his native land.

---

[1] Micah 5:2 NIV

Most good stories have a twist. Daniel's story has a twist, but he won't live to see its fulfillment. A role will be forced upon Daniel. As he succeeds in his new position in a foreign land, he will impact two major empires. He will even reach twenty-five hundred years into the future to touch an event in our world. It might not have happened if Daniel had not learned to grow in his knowledge of God. In time, he will gain a unique identification even on the same level as the New Testament apostle John, who was called the beloved apostle.

> **Daniel 10:11 (KJV)** – *He said unto me, O Daniel, **a man greatly beloved**, understand the words that I speak unto thee, and stand upright: for unto thee am I now sent. And when he had spoken this word unto me, I stood trembling.*

The thought-provoking idea is when you are considered God's friend; he reveals his plans in-depth. Jesus follows this example when he says servants don't know their master's business. "But I call you friends, for everything I learn from the Father, I share these things with you" (John 15:15). John, the apostle, wrote the book of Revelation. In the same vein, Daniel will tell some of the same events hundreds of years before John is born. It starts with a dream.

Interpreting Dreams

We all have dreams, but we don't all expect God to speak to us through dreams. When the prophet Joel says the Holy Spirit will be poured out on all flesh, we write sermons and encourage believers that the promises of God are true and faithful. When the same prophet tells us our sons and daughters will prophesy and young men will have vision and old men will dream dreams (Joel 2:28), We wonder how that works or is it relevant or meaningful? We don't know what to say about visions and dreams unless we are trained to see how other biblical prophets handle such experiences.

When the need to interpret dreams are thrust upon you, do what Daniel did and pray. Why? Because often God is the only one who knows what is really going on. Here's how the story unfolds in Daniel's life. "So the king summoned the magicians, enchanters, sorcerers, and astrologers to tell him what he had dreamed. When they came in and stood before the king, he said to them, 'I have had a dream that troubles me, and I want to know what it means."[2]

"Then the astrologers answered the king, 'May the king live forever! Tell your servants the dream, and we will interpret it.' The king replied to the astrologers, 'This is what I have firmly decided: If you do not tell me what my dream was and interpret it, I will have you cut into pieces, and your houses turned into piles of rubble. But if you tell me the dream and explain it, you will receive from me gifts and rewards and great honor. So tell me the dream and interpret it for me."[3]

The king did not trust the group of advisors, for most of them were from his father's reign. He wanted to put what seemed like an impossible task on these wise men and offered compelling incentives. This group of advisors, magicians,

---

[2]   Daniel 2:2-3 NIV

[3]   Daniel 2:4-6 NIV

enchanters, sorcerers, and astrologers went back and forth with the king about the petition to tell them what the dream was all about. The king wanted someone who knew things nobody else could understand. Isn't that what we all want from God? The king didn't realize that Daniel's God was listening. But God is always listening and looking for opportunities to reveal himself and his power. 'If you do not tell me what I dreamed, there is only one penalty for you. You have conspired to tell me misleading and wicked things, hoping the situation will change. So then, tell me the dream, and I will know that you can interpret it for me.' The astrologers answered the king, 'There is no one on earth who can do what the king asks! No king, however great and mighty, has ever asked such a thing of any magician or enchanter or astrologer. What the king asks is too difficult. No one can reveal it to the king except the gods, and they do not live among humans.' This made the king so angry and furious that he ordered the execution of all the wise men of Babylon. The decree was issued to put the wise men to death, and men were sent to look for Daniel and his friends to put them to death."[4]

Now Daniel and his three friends have been out of the loop on this conversation with the King. They only get the news that they are to be executed along with the wise men of Babylon for failure to grant the King his request. Daniel reveals his leadership skills by taking over the situation and working out a deal with the king's soldier to allow them a night to interpret the king's dream. Daniel calls for an all-night prayer meeting. During the night,

---

[4] Daniel 2:9-13 NIV

the mystery of the king's dream is revealed to him in a vision. The next day, Daniel meets with Nebuchadnezzar and what he says to the king will provide insight into the future of several empires that will rule the world—a prophetic dream through a pagan king. Daniel 2:27-29 – Daniel replied, "No wise man, enchanter, magician or diviner can explain to the king the mystery he has asked about, but there is a God in heaven who reveals mysteries. He has shown King Nebuchadnezzar what will happen in days to come. Your dream and the visions that passed through your mind as you were lying in bed are these: As Your Majesty was lying there, your mind turned to things to come, and the revealer of mysteries showed you what is going to happen."

Don't miss the importance that Daniel refused to accept the credit or, more importantly, the glory for his revelation to King Nebuchadnezzar. What a powerful truth it is that God in heaven reveals mysteries; we can only be a conduit. A person who accepts the call to be a prophet must never forget the source is never a man or woman. God is the only one who is all-knowing. When God shares that knowledge with his children through Scriptures, visions, or dreams, they must give the glory and credit to him. Daniel's obedience to God and his loyalty to a pagan king eventually becomes a game changer. "Your Majesty looked, and there before you stood a large statue—an enormous, dazzling statue, awesome in appearance. The head of the statue was made of pure gold, its chest and arms of silver, its belly, and thighs of bronze, its legs of iron, its feet partly of iron and partly of baked clay. While you were watching, a rock was cut out, but not by human hands. It struck the statue on its feet of iron and clay and smashed them. Then the iron, the clay, the bronze, the silver, and the gold were all broken to pieces and became like chaff on a threshing floor in the summer. The wind swept them away without leaving a trace. But the rock that struck the statue became a huge mountain and filled the whole earth.[5] This was the dream, and now we will interpret it to the king."

Daniel's descriptions of Nebuchadnezzar's empire and then the empires that ruled the world following the Babylonians have been documented as the most accurate insight to what will happen in the world over the next five hundred years, and it astounds historians. The king's decision because of this interpretation is the focus of every generation of Christians since. Your church has probably performed a Christmas play because of the result of the interpretation of Nebuchadnezzar dream. "The king said to Daniel, 'Surely your God is the God of gods and the Lord of kings and a revealer of mysteries, for you were able to reveal this mystery.' Then the king placed Daniel in a high position and lavished many gifts on him. He made him ruler over the entire province of Babylon and placed him in charge of all its **wise men.**"[6]

The Wise Guys

The wise men that Daniel was placed over had a lot of identities and skills. When my son Chris was in grade school, he announced to everyone he would be one of the wise guys in the Christmas children's play. The Christmas wise men are descendants of the men that Daniel was put in charge of, but

---

5   Daniel 2:31-36 NIV

6   Daniel 2:47-48 NIV

not all of them were wise or even good. In the Babylon Empire, they honored all sources of information—a lot like we do in our society today. You, too, could be considered an advisor to a king or governor of a region if you had the skills. The position of an advisor, had honed skills such as interpreting dreams and skills in the sciences such as astronomy and astrology. Even sorcery and witchcraft were sought after. Daniel was placed over this mixed bag of people, but historians believe he weeded out of the group the evil and less desirable people as advisors. The wise men, in time, became people who were godly in counsel, had skills in the sciences of astronomy and astrology, and possessed the ability to interpret dreams. These skills enabled the wise men to interpret the signs of Jesus coming into the world as a baby.

The Bethlehem Star

With a star as their main clue, how were the astronomers and astrologers able to anticipate a coming King? What did they see or what information was given to them as a map? The group known as wise men from the east followed that star. They are called wise men in Matthew 2, traveling all the way from Babylon, reading the clues and considering the heavens. It was not an overnight trip; it would take a two-year journey before they found Jesus in the town of Bethlehem. Some say it's just an ancient story about a star. Is it a myth? You can follow the science to learn the many details that reveal what the Bethlehem star really is. You might not believe it, but the secular news and scientists provided the best explanation when the Bethlehem star appeared in the summer of 2015. **"Star of Bethlehem"** Visible on June 30th for the First Time in 2,000 Years. "On June 30th,

Jupiter and Venus merged into what is known as a super-star. The conjunction of these two planets has been building throughout the month of June, and the result will be a dazzling bright display spectacular on June 30th." said NASA in a news release. "On that night [June 30] Venus and Jupiter will be a ... 1/3rd of a degree apart. That's less than the diameter of a full moon. You'll be able to hide the pair not just behind the palm of your outstretched hand, but behind your little pinky finger," added NASA.[7]

Venus and Jupiter [8]

Sky and telescope suggests that a similar rare conjunction of Venus and Jupiter may have been what was known as the "Star

---

[7] Nasa news release (June 30, 2015).

[8] "Venus & Jupiter to pair in spectacular 'Star of Bethlehem' conjunction," (Nasa published news release time: 30 Jun 2015, 11:43).

of Bethlehem" in 3–2 BC, and since then, there has not been a brighter, closer planetary conjunction. That means that this is the first opportunity of seeing it so clear for 2,000 years![9]

Science gives us the first clue; stars don't move but, planets do! The cool part is Jupiter is known as the king planet, and Venus is known as the planet of love. You put them together, and you've got the king of love sign from the heavens. Now that's a story that should be told every Christmas. Thanks to the prophet Daniel who prepared wise men to pass this kind of information down for five hundred years until the planets could align to guide them to the newborn baby Jesus.

The appearing of this star took place two summers in a row 2015 and 2016. Are these the signs Jesus talked about regarding his second coming in Luke 21? We are enjoying the unfolding of prophecy that many generations of Christians have waited to see. I can't guarantee Jesus is returning on a specific date. But his star has already reappeared, and what a joy it was to share the experience in 2015 with my youngest son Chris. As we stood together looking at the Star of Bethlehem on June 30, 2015, we wondered what it could mean for our futures.

God's knowledge and insight were handed down from generation to generation without flaw or error. Even though we don't have a record of the instructions the wise men were given, we have the results of their expertise in our New Testament account of Jesus's birth in Matthew Chapter Two, where they bring their gifts and worship the son of God.

---

[9] Judith Kelly, "Venus and Jupiter Together at Last," Skyandtelescope.com, (June 25, 2015).

CHAPTER 11

Sleeping Beauty (The Church)

There are many parallels between the story of Sleeping Beauty and the church, such as the many blessings bestowed upon her by good fairies and a curse with a prophecy of her death from a wicked fairy.

Sleeping Beauty by Charles Perrault (1959 Disney Film)

Once upon a time, there lived a king and queen who were very unhappy because they had no children. But at last a daughter was born, and their sorrow turned to joy. The king gave a christening feast, and at the end of the feast, the youngest fairy stepped forward and said, "The princess shall be the most beautiful woman in the world." The second said, "She shall have a temper as sweet as an angel." The third said, "She shall have a wonderful grace in all she does or says." The fourth said, "She shall sing like a nightingale." The fifth said, "She shall dance like a flower in the wind." The sixth said, "She shall play such music as was never heard on earth." Then the old fairy's turn came. Shaking her head spitefully, she said, "When the princess is seventeen years old, she shall prick her finger with a spindle, and she shall die!" All the guests trembled, and many of them began to weep. The king and queen wept loudest of all.[1]

Has the church, the people of God, lost its calling to the world and became a "Sleeping Beauty"? Did the church prick a finger on the culture of desire, wanting so much to be accepted and perceived as normal? Did the fears and accusations about our faith and obedience make us feel vulnerable? Did we make an unconscious decision to refuse to be seen as the ugly step-sister of society? Our uniqueness was once how God transformed people into his bride called the church, and now we clothe ourselves in the likeness of a world. There is a prophecy of our beauty being restored. "It was given to her to clothe herself in fine linen, bright and clean; for the fine linen is the righteous acts of the saints."[2]

Blessings and curses are a part of this fallen world. The church is not exempt from the consequences of the sin. We are vulnerable to the spells of media and culture. Sleeping Beauty's curse didn't bring her death, but a deep sleep and for one hundred years, she waited to be revived with the kiss of life. In the same way, the church must receive a fresh touch or a holy kiss. Jesus gives reassurance that his beauty will be blameless and without spot or wrinkle.[3]

In the Old Testament, whenever Israel fell asleep in their faith or was lured by the other nations to dabble in cultural sins of their day, God sent a prophet to warn them of the consequences of their

---

[1] Charles Perrault, *Sleeping Beauty*, (1959).

[2] Revelation 19:18 NIV

[3] Ephesians 5:27 NIV

choices. God is the same yesterday, today, and forever more. I have noticed the voice of the prophet returning to our pulpits and even in our streets. Young men and women are using social media to redeem the times. Boldness and holiness are coming to a church near you. Do you have ears to hear the message?

A Noisy World

God will speak through the prophet when one is available. If there isn't one, he communicates through vision and dreams, through circumstances, or open and closed doors. But if you're sleeping, it doesn't matter what method of communication is used. Since you are asleep, you won't understand what's being said or see what's taking place. The church has pricked its finger on the spindle of the culture and relevancy and has fallen deep asleep, and its mission and the great commission are hibernating. The church has been asleep for more than fifty years. We saw prayer removed from the public sector in the 60s, and abortion became the law of the land. In the 70s and in 2015, the assault was against babies and marriage as we handed them over to the enemy. The culture is more highly valued than a sacred gift given to a man and woman by God. While the church is sleeping, we may snore through the second coming of Jesus. He warns the church of Sardis of this problem and gives them some frightening truths. The first, something within the body is about to die.[4] Jesus's words are spellbinding as he calls the church several times to wake up. Even amid all the noise and Jesus's promptings, the church continues to sleep.

---

[4]   Revelation 3:2 NIV

Waking Up the Church

Don't be found sleeping when God is talking. Prophetic scriptures point to God using creation to communicate to us in the last days. Our biblical puzzle is not just a picture of the earth but of the whole creation. God's signs for us are not done in secret. Matthew 24:29 says; "Immediately after the distress of those days" 'the sun will be darkened, and the moon will not give its light; the stars will fall from the sky, and the heavenly bodies will be shaken." So many of the prophets write about the events in the heavens—Isaiah, Daniel, Joel, Amos, Job, Ezekiel, Jeremiah, and even Moses in the Old Testament. The heavens declaring the message of God is something we learned in Sunday School; within the Christmas story, we learned of the arrival of the wise men following the star. I am afraid we are becoming so earthly minded in our faith that we cannot hear the heavens speaking, but it doesn't mean they aren't talking to us. King David proclaimed, "The heavens declare the glory of God; the skies proclaim the work of his hands. Day after day they pour forth speech; night after night they reveal knowledge. They have no speech, they use no words; no sound is heard from them. Yet their voice goes out into all the earth, their words to the ends of the world. In the heavens, God has pitched a tent for the sun."[5]

The messages have been coming from the heavens loud and clear for several years. Blood red moons appeared two years in a row on the Jewish holidays of Passover and Tabernacles in 2015 and 2016. Also, the Bethlehem Star has appeared two summers in a row during 2015, 2016. We need to wake up from our slumber

---

[5]   Psalm 19:1-4 NIV

and get caught up in what God is saying from the heavens. The messages behind these appearances seem to be warnings or, at best, God is trying to get the attention of those who believed his words, and even the world is experiencing perplexity at the roaring and tossing of the sea. Just this summer, Texas and Florida were shaken by the hurricanes that struck them, and the billions of dollars of damage mystified the scientific community.

Research on the four blood red moons has given me the confidence to say, "The message was more for the nation of Israel than for the church community. Two years in a row a lunar eclipse, a blood red moon on Passover and then again on Tabernacles represents the first feast and the last feast. The beginning and the end, the first and the last are the words of Jesus. "'I am the Alpha and the Omega,' says the Lord God, 'who is, and who was, and who is to come, the Almighty.'⁶ What a beautiful personal note from Jesus himself to the Jewish people about who he is and what he is about to do. Passover and Tabernacles are two of the three major feasts in Judaism, with the middle feast being Pentecost. All three feasts required males to go to their place of birth and honor God with a sacrifice. Sadly, Israel has also been asleep a long time, and they are missing the significance of God using the first and the last feast to speak to the world about his return.

Eclipse

At the end of January 2018, a total lunar eclipse happened on a rare blue moon. Before this, an extraordinary solar eclipse occurred in summer 2017 and traveled across the United States.

---

⁶ Revelation 1:8 NIV

In a Christian news report, the announcer said, "The people of the United States were excited about this event; is it possible that God is speaking from the heavens using the sun and the moon to communicate?" Yes, but the church has been sleeping, and no one is telling the people. Jesus said in Luke 21 and Matthew 24 there would be signs in the sun, moon, and stars. Therefore, we have awe without enlightenment.

During the solar eclipse, millions of Americans were converging on a narrow corridor stretching from Oregon to South Carolina to watch the moon blot out the midday sun. For a wondrous couple of minutes in the first total solar eclipse to sweep coast to coast in 99 years. Veteran eclipse watchers warned the uninitiated to get ready to be blown away by its rarity. Planetariums and museums posted "Sold out of eclipse glasses" on their front doors. Signs along highways reminded motorists of "Solar Eclipse Monday," while cars bore the message "Eclipse or bust." With 200 million people within a day's drive of the path of totality, towns and parks braced for monumental crowds. It's expected to be the most observed, most studied, and most photographed eclipse ever. Not to mention the most festive, what with all the parties. In Salem, Oregon, a field outside the state fairgrounds was transformed into a campground in advance of an eclipse-watching party for 8,500.[7]

The data that has come out about what it takes to pull off a total solar eclipse is evidence of a Master of the universe. The sun is four hundred times larger than our moon, but the moon is exactly four hundred times closer to the earth than it is the sun.

---

[7] Marcia Dunn, August 20, 2017, https://stream.org.

The precision that went into the customizing of the universe, just so we could see a total eclipse is terrific evidence of our Creator. The moon's orbit pattern around the earth is the only orbit that would allow a total eclipse with our sun.

The Digital Information Age

Most of us have the latest technology, and I for one would not want to be without it. However, many believers find it easier to trust digital information than to trust the signs in the heavens. It seems God speaking from the heavens is a difficult message for them to embrace. But, in fact, Scripture indicated long ago that what we are witnessing is a fulfillment of prophecy.

Daniel's prophecy about Jesus's second coming is more informative about the mysteries of Jesus's return, especially pertaining to the timing. Details about the period we have entered are obvious. Daniel was instructed to seal up the writings until a certain time described regarding a great advancement in civilization. "But you, Daniel, roll up and seal the words of the scroll until the time of the end. Many will go here and there to increase knowledge."[8]

Many will go here and there. In the last seventy years, plane travel makes this prophecy possible. Maybe you are one of the everyday travelers that do your business by plane. You probably never thought of yourself as one of the many fulfilling Daniel's prophecies.

(July 31, 2017) Every minute, every hour, every day, there are men and women at work. Flights handled by the FAA ...

---

[8]   Daniel 12:4 NIV

2,586,582 domestic/international passengers fly every day. 26,527 average daily scheduled flights.[9]

The ability to travel has exploded in this generation. If we added the people that are traveling by car, bus, or train to the already two and a half million people traveling by plane. This would grow to 488 million people who travel for business each year in or to the United States alone.[10] The prophecy also describes when knowledge will increase. Daniel 12:4 is where you can examine the accuracy of these events.

Different Types of Knowledge Have Different Rates of Growth

On average, human knowledge is doubling every thirteen months. According to IBM, "The build-out of the 'internet of things' will lead to the doubling of knowledge every twelve hours."

Online info doubles every six months.
Biological info doubles every eighteen months.
Corporate info doubles every eighteen months.
Genetic info doubles every eighteen months.
Technical knowledge doubles every twelve months.
Clinical knowledge doubles every eighteen months.[11]

---

[9] Air Traffic by the Numbers, faa.gov.

[10] Ibid

[11] Patrice Lewis, "Is Knowledge Doubling?", mbil.wind.com.

Patrice Lewis says, "With this kind of speed, these facts and figures are changing. We can all agree that knowledge and the increasing of it are staggering." We have a catch twenty-two in that when knowledge is king, we can make information say almost anything we want it to. When considering how slow news developed or knowledge increased prior to the twentieth century, I can safely say this is an on-target prophecy. This end times knowledge has changed the ability to be bold. Today's prophets have so much more insight available to them, and the internet was a game changer. It allows me to find answers and research passages with such speed that it would have taken me a lifetime to do without it.

Israel Is Waking Up

Many want to know how the end time events will unfold. The exciting fact is before 1948, all of it was speculation. Preachers for 1,873 years had a missing piece to the puzzle of Jesus's second coming. Without a nation called Israel, how could the fulfillment of so many Scriptures happen? It couldn't! You and I are living in the age of Ezekiel's prophecy of dry bones living again. One historian said after World War II, the Jewish people who returned to Israel looked like skeletons, for many of them were skin and bones. Then after being attacked in 1967 by three countries that should have soundly defeated the young nation of Israel. Except for God's intervention in the six days war, another piece of the puzzle would not have been added to the picture. Jerusalem once again was under Israel's control. Jesus told us when you see the fig tree blossom, you will know that the time is near. Any interpretation of last days without a fully restored state of Israel and God's sovereign plan for them will fall short of understanding end-times prophecy. In a strange way, the nation of Israel seems to be more aware of the season and the times than the followers of Jesus. I am continually impressed with Prime Minister Benjamin Netanyahu's appeal to believers and his love for our beliefs.

Shaken but Not Stirred

As the church is getting more missional in caring about the poor and injustice, which are good things for us to address, it can be in danger of missing the heart of Jesus. Jesus said, "The poor you will always have with you."[12] He wasn't saying this to weaken ministry to the poor. On the contrary, when placed in context, we see it was all about preparing for his death and burial. This is not an either/or proposition but a call to not miss the timing of these events. Culture has shaped the church more than most leaders are willing to admit. We so desire to have the approval of man it affects how we think, act, and come across to our society. This goes against the teaching of Jesus, who did not bend to the pressures of his day—neither in the religious sense nor a politically correct narrative. Jesus came to change the whole world system by establishing a kingdom way of life. The church is not often in a kingdom pattern. The kingdom won't resemble this world's priorities. What stirs the heart of the church in the 21st century does not align with God's heart. A Christian who doesn't understand the times will not know what to do in those times. Wake up, Church, and sense where the Spirit of God

---

[12] Matthew 26:11 NIV

is leading his people. I love the romance and intrigue in the story of Sleeping Beauty. God is a romantic who is always the pursuer, calling to humanity with his love and promises. Some may think I have a silly, romantic view of prophecy. Could the prophetic letters be notes and clues left by our God? Does he smile when we are awakened to a clue about his love and desire for us? I can only hope so.

CHAPTER 12

Beyond Literature

On December 6, 2013, Dr. Scott Carroll, an ancient manuscript specialist, was ready to announce his findings. Layers of papyrus dating between the third century B.C. and fifth century A.D. had been tediously extracted and identified from a rare Egyptian burial site. They found six ancient New Testament passages and one Old Testament manuscript fragment in all seven treasures. These could be the earliest papyrus passages ever recorded.[1]

In a day when megachurches are declaring we put too much emphasis on the Word of God, why would men like Dr. Scott Carroll and Josh McDowell be so excited about the evidence of passages from the Gospels and the Old Testament? Something more than ancient history is being discovered; it's the validation of the importance of Scripture shared in the early church, which took painstaking measures to pass on the words of Jesus. Eyewitness accounts are just one portion of the story of the Bible. The living and active Word of God is at the core of Christianity. The argument is too many Christians are Bible students and not

---

[1]   Josh McDowell, *God-Breathed*, (2015), 29.

doers of the Word. I fully understand the word must move from our mind and into our spirit and from there into our obedience. The Scripture promises to do the work as it gets inside of us! It is sharper than any double-edged sword with the ability to divide our thoughts and attitudes.[2] The words on the page are not the origin of a human author. The words themselves hold blessings. Those who read the words of this prophecy out loud are blessed, and those who hear those words read and take them to heart are blessed.[3] No other book can make this claim other than the Bible. God issues a warning that if you change by adding or taking away from this scroll, God will take away the tree of life.[4] He put a "Beware" label on the Bible warning those who will read it.

Could these warnings be what made the scriptural accuracy so crucial to our evidence of inerrancy? The scribes would take hours to be precise in their copying, so they could pass them on to each other. Can we get into the mindset of those entrusted with such a task? As a Catholic boy who wasn't encouraged to own a Bible, I have a personal answer to the question. When you own a Bible, you have a tangible part of God always with you. The God, who people question is real or if he cares, gave us a piece of eternity in the Scriptures—the Holy Word of God. I remember as a young man, we never placed anything on our Bible out of reverence for it. Some say people make it an idol. Yet God says one day everything will come under judgment except

---

[2] Hebrews 4:12 NIV

[3] Revelation 1:3 NIV

[4] Revelation 22:19 NIV

his Word, for it will abide and endures forever.[5] The apostle Paul reminds us they were not written with human wisdom but with the Spirit, and only the Spirit-filled people have the discernment to grasp its kingdom nature.[6]

Be careful never to place the Scripture in a category of only being historical. This classification, though, does apply in one sense because it is history. It can never be the ultimate view because our God is alive and so is his Word. It continues to invigorate you by the Holy Spirit and has been doing so for more than three thousand years. It will remain alive for the eons of time.[7]

The Single-Mindedness of the Word

My oldest son Shawn is a lead pastor in Missouri, and I love when he calls me about a problem. It often has a personal edge or sharpness. I listen and give a lot of okays and I understand, or oh this happens to every pastor answers. Then I remind him of how the Scripture says we should act, respond, and think and that love covers a multitude of sins.[8] In many ways, I lay down the law on being a pastor. Ouch, and then the Holy Spirit convicts me. We must act differently because of the Spirit not because of the law. Why do we so quickly dish out the law? Paul tells us the law

---

[5] I Peter 1:25 NIV

[6] I Corinthians 2:13-14 NIV

[7] Josh McDowell, *God-Breathed*, 35.

[8] I Peter 4:8 NIV

brings death and only the Spirit can bring life.[9] My son knows the Scripture as well if not better than I. He is not calling to get a lesson in the law but in the Spirit. Boundaries are healthy and understanding the difference between good and evil is a must. The light within the Word of God always points to the God who is relational. I know God is also missional, but the key to the mission is the relationship. His single-mindedness is about the relationship.

Personal Interpretation

Every Sunday School class, home group, and Bible study has heard this phrase: This passage means this to me. We even go around the circle at times asking people to share what it means to them.

There are two fundamental mistakes people make when they try to interpret the Bible.

1. They inject their own views or emotions into the Scripture.
2. They take a verse, word, or phrase out of context.[10]

This may sound like a contradiction to what I just wrote earlier, but nothing in the Scripture was written *directly to you or me*. Some Scriptures were written directly to other people, and some Scriptures were written with humanity in mind since God

---

[9] Romans 5:20-21 NIV

[10] Josh McDowell, *God-Breathed*, 54.

is all-knowing. Remember, the Word is a living record detailing God's heart and Spirit to a world he created. You can have a personal application without having a personal interpretation. The key difference is when we read the Bible, we enter God's kingdom. It's his Spirit realm or tangible part of him we are connecting with throughout history. God living outside of time makes his Word timeless in the spiritual sense but not in the historical. The best rule of thumb is to look for God's consistency, or like my friend Rabbi Herb said, The Hebrew pattern will show the witness of God's heart on a subject.

Trustworthiness

I live in a University area where the latest information is considered sacred, and I hear a lot of "You're not trusting those passages are you?" The test for the reliability of Scripture stands up more significantly than many of the historical works of secular books that have fewer copies of the original work than most of our Scriptures.

There are presently 5,686 Greek manuscripts in existence today for the New Testament. If we compared the number of New Testament manuscripts to other ancient writings, we'd find that the New Testament manuscripts far outweigh the others in quantity.[11]

---

[11] Tom Slick, "Manuscript Evidence of Superior New Testament Reliability," (Dec. 10, 2008).

Author	Date Written	Earliest Copy	Approximate Time Span between Original & Copy	Number of Copies	Accuracy of Copies
Lucretius	died 55 or 53 B.C.		1100 yrs.	2	----
Pliny	A.D. 61-113	A.D. 850	750 yrs.	7	----
Plato	427-347 B.C.	A.D. 900	1200 yrs.	7	----
Demosthenes	4th Cent. B.C.	A.D. 1100	800 yrs.	8	----
Herodotus	480-425 B.C.	A.D. 900	1300 yrs.	8	----
Suetonius	A.D. 75-160	A.D. 950	800 yrs.	8	----
Thucydides	460-400 B.C.	A.D. 900	1300 yrs.	8	----
Euripides	480-406 B.C.	A.D. 1100	1300 yrs.	9	----
Aristophanes	450-385 B.C.	A.D. 900	1200	10	----
Caesar	100-44 B.C.	A.D. 900	1000	10	----
Livy	59 BC-AD 17	----	???	20	----
Tacitus	circa A.D. 100	A.D. 1100	1000 yrs.	20	----
Aristotle	384-322 B.C.	A.D. 1100	1400	49	----
Sophocles	496-406 B.C.	A.D. 1000	1400 yrs.	193	----
Homer (Iliad)	900 B.C.	400 B.C.	500 yrs.	643	95%
New Testament	1st Cent. A.D. (A.D. 50-100)	2nd Cent. A.D. (c. A.D. 130 f.)	less than 100 years	5600	99.5%

Literature Graph[12]

Many are trying to discredit the Scriptures when its trustworthiness far outweighs other works. This leads me to believe the enemy who seeks to steal, kill, and destroy is busy

---

[12] Tom Slick, "Manuscript Evidence of Superior New Testament Reliability" and graph, (Dec. 10, 2008).

carrying out his agenda.[13] Since the Holy Spirit is the author of the Bible, we can rest in the fact that the Bible is without error. I have referenced Josh McDowell several times and suggest reading his book called *God-Breathed*. He uses inordinate detail as an apologetic to approach the reliability of the Scriptures. As a simple application, I ask the question? If the Bible has errors in it would God want a flawed book around for eternity?

The Power of the Word

The attacks on the Word of God are assaults on God's power. Have you ever come across someone who is proud that they read Bible through every year? I am not sure who said this, but it has stuck with me. It's not how much of the Bible you've gone through; it's how much has gotten inside of you. The devil knows the power of the Word and twisted it while trying to tempt Jesus in the wilderness. Jesus displayed the power of the Word when used correctly by rebuking the devil with Scripture. Holy Scriptures minus the Holy Spirit equals bibliolatry.[14] The work of the Holy Spirit is to point to the truth and to convict us when we are living in deception. He continues to be a faithful helper, so we can know, live, and grow in kingdom realities. I love the book of Romans for many reasons but one reason in particular, is its use of the phrase "For we know," and "We know." The lyrics of a great hymn by Daniel Whittle state, "I know Whom I have believed, and am persuaded that He is able to keep that which I've committed unto Him against that day."

---

[13] John 10:10 NIV

[14] Mark Batterson, *Whisper*, 67

Active/Functional

You can live without being functional or active. The Scripture boasts, and make no mistake, it is a boast, that God's Word is living and active. In the Greek translation of the word active, it means to be at work or to energize. Why do so many people claim that reading the Word is boring or they don't get anything out of it? We often want the Word of God to make us feel better or to help us emotionally. I believe these desires can be valid, but we are missing the point of writings coming from God. He wants to activate your soul to function, so you can operate as a spirit-filled, spirit-led person. For your mind to comprehend this way of living, you must surrender it to the washing of the Word and for an upgrade to the kingdom program. The viruses of the old operating system are stilling trying to play in your mind, are the world's programs. Paul reminds us the old system is dysfunctional and dangerous, even deadly. The Word of God is designed to integrate our intellect and emotions to a new Spirit level of processing life. The digital age is a great example of how fast something can change. In the same way, a person can change rapidly if they submit to the Spirit's leading in their life. As I read the Word, I am looking for new areas where the Scriptures can reprogram my soul, mind, and even my emotions to the Spirit-filled life.

Beyond

Bill Easum and Dave Travis wrote a book titled *Beyond the Box*. It is a look at the church box thinking and beyond.[15] It's time

---

[15] Bill Easum and Dave Travis, *Beyond the Box,* 71.

to think of the Bible in a category beyond literature. Its essence is more than words; it is dimensional in ways we might not fully understand until the veil is removed and we are in eternity. Since God is keeping his Word around for eternity, the purposes and insights could continue to be realized. Could Jesus use the Word of God to set up his government in the new millennium? When God creates the new heaven and new earth, will he tell us to turn to Genesis 1 as we watch him create once again? When the Bible calls the Word of God living and active, how can we limit it to the category of literature alone? Our finite minds have a hard time grasping all the infinite wonders God has in store for us. Some of those wonders we won't have to wait until heaven to see. They are being realized through the fulfillment of Scripture almost every day.

Does shrinking God down to our understanding start with shrinking the potential of his Word? So many questions, and I know we can only speculate on the answers. But wow, did you just feel it? Can you sense it in your spirit? Embracing the Word of God as truth expands our imagination, and, in that instant, we've met the All-Knowing.